S Corporation
ESOPs

Third Edition

S Corporation
ESOPs

Third Edition

David Ackerman
Kathryn F. Aschwald
Barbara M. Clough
Renee Lewis
Anthony I. Mathews
Thomas Roback, Jr.
Corey Rosen
Donna J. Walker
Carolyn F. Zimmerman

The National Center for Employee Ownership
Oakland, California

S Corporation ESOPs, 3rd ed.

Book design and editing by Scott Rodrick

The National Center for Employee Ownership
1736 Franklin St., 8th Floor
Oakland, CA 94612
(510) 208-1300
Fax (510) 272-9510
www.nceo.org

First edition, July 2004; second edition, October 2005; third edition, March 2008

ISBN-10: 1-932924-45-0
ISBN-13: 978-1-932924-45-9

Contents

Preface

An employee stock ownership plan (ESOP) is a powerful tool that can greatly benefit both employees and their employer. When an ESOP owns an S corporation, it is partially or wholly exempt from federal income taxation (and possibly state taxation, depending on the state), making it an even more powerful tool in many cases. With the tax-planning possibilities offered by the S corporation ESOP structure, many companies are investigating ESOPs and S corporate status. But there are many issues to deal with along the way, ranging from valuation issues to matters that arise when making the S corporation election (if the company is not already an S corporation) to dealing with the unavailability of the tax-deferred ESOP "rollover" for S corporation owners. Most importantly, however, it is imperative for any company considering or maintaining an S corporation ESOP to test its compliance with the strict anti-abuse rules for S corporation ESOPs.

This book deals with all these issues and more in a clear and understandable style. This third edition has been updated to deal with recent developments, with every chapter revised to some extent, and two new chapters added: chapter 3, "A State-by-State Analysis of S Corporation Tax Treatment," and chapter 7, "Phantom Stock and SARs in S Corporation ESOP Companies."

How S Corporation ESOPs Came to Be

Corey Rosen

The idea of employee ownership can be traced back to the 18th century in the U.S., and since then various plans have been set up to encourage employees to buy stock in their employer or for employers to share ownership. But none of these approaches gained widespread use. Meanwhile, ownership was concentrating in fewer and fewer hands.

In the 1950s, a San Francisco investment banker and attorney named Louis Kelso devised a way to use employee benefit plan trusts to borrow money to buy company shares. Companies could get a tax deduction for repaying the loan through the trust. Kelso called the idea an ESOP, for employee stock ownership plan. He persuaded several companies to set up the plans, but they needed case-by-case approval from the IRS. By 1973, however, he had persuaded the chair of the Senate Finance Committee, Senator Russell Long (D-La), that ESOPs should receive formal statutory support. In 1974, Long persuaded his colleagues that the idea had merit. That year, Congress was reforming retirement plan law through legislation that would be known as the Employee Retirement Income Security Act (ERISA). Because that bill was sure to pass, and because ESOPs generally fit under many of its concepts, ESOPs became part of ERISA. As a result, ESOPs are subject to many of the same rules as pension funds, 401(k) plans, stock bonus plans, and profit sharing plans.

In addition to allowing the corporate tax deduction for contributions a company made to an ESOP (to repay an ESOP loan or just as a straight cash or stock contribution), ERISA requires ESOPs to be invested primarily in company stock, although diversification could be required if those responsible for the plans know or should know

1

that the investment is not prudent. That protects plan fiduciaries from being sued for lack of diversification, as they easily could be in other retirement plans.

Over the next 25 years, Congress added many more tax benefits to encourage employee ownership, most notably (and chronologically):

- Providing sponsors of ESOPs that borrow money with higher contribution limits than other plans (since 2001, however, other plan limits have been raised to match the ESOP limits).

- Allowing sellers of stock to an ESOP in a C corporation to defer taxation on the gain made from the sale by reinvesting in other securities if the ESOP ends up owning at least 30% of the shares.

- Making dividends paid to an ESOP tax-deductible if they are used to repay the ESOP loan, are passed through directly to employees, or are used by employees to reinvest in company stock.

- Providing that an ESOP could own stock in an S corporation and that any federal income tax attributable to the plan's ownership would not be subject to federal income tax.

All of these laws, however, applied only to C corporations. Thanks in no small measure (but not solely) to these tax benefits, ESOPs grew quickly. Until 1998, all these incentives were terrific—if you were a C corporation. S corporations could not have ESOPs because until 1998, nontaxable entities of any kind could not own S corporations. In an S corporation, profits are not taxed at the corporate level. Instead, individual owners pay tax on their pro-rata shares of earnings. If an entity with a tax rate of zero were an owner, then it would not pay any tax. Effective January 1, 1998, as part of a broad reform of S corporation laws enacted in 1996, ESOPs and other nontaxable entities became eligible to be S corporation owners. However, under the initial 1996 legislation, they would have to pay income tax, generally at the top marginal rates. In 1997, Congress amended the law before it became effective to provide that ESOPs, and only ESOPs, were exempt from this tax requirement. So if an ESOP owns 30% of an S corporation, 30% of the company's profits are not taxed at the federal level; if the ESOP owns 100% of an S corporation, none of the company's earnings are taxed at the federal level. As a matter of existing law, moreover, the ESOP is considered a single shareholder, no matter how many participants the ESOP has. That is potentially important because S corporations are limited to 100 owners.

The new law had two immediate effects. First, some S corporations decided to set up new ESOPs. Second, many existing C corporation ESOPs moved quickly to 100% ESOP ownership so that they could get the full benefit of this special tax break. As generous as the law is, however, some special tax benefits of ESOPs do not apply to S corporations. Most importantly, sellers to an S corporation ESOP cannot defer taxation on profits made from the sale. In addition, S corporations cannot deduct dividends used to repay an ESOP loan, passed through to ESOP participants, or voluntarily reinvested in company stock by ESOP participants (although they can use distributions to help repay the debt). In C corporations, interest used to repay the ESOP debt generally does not count against the limitations on what can be contributed to a plan; in S corporations, it does. Unlike C corporations, S corporations also cannot delay distributions to former participants until after the debt is repaid. Some of the differences may have been unintentional, but there is little immediate prospect of their being added to S corporation ESOP advantages.

Given the magnitude of the S corporation ESOP tax benefits, of course, it is not surprising that some people have tried to abuse the rules by setting up plans with little or no benefit to ordinary employees. Congress and the IRS, with the full support from the ESOP community, have cracked down on these schemes with stringent anti-abuse rules for S corporation ESOPs.

The first chapter of this book looks at how ESOPs work in general. The following chapters address the various special rules and issues for S corporation ESOPs, including the anti-abuse rules mentioned above. The final chapter addresses how ESOP companies can create true ownership cultures.

CHAPTER ONE

How ESOPs Work

Corey Rosen

An ESOP is a kind of employee benefit plan. Governed by ERISA (the Employee Retirement Income Security Act), ESOPs were given a specific statutory framework in 1974. ESOPs are similar in many ways to 401(k) plans and profit sharing plans. All of these plans operate through a trust, require that their benefits be provided on a nondiscriminatory basis to employees, and provide both the sponsoring employer and the employee with significant tax benefits. Unlike 401(k) plans, however, ESOPs are almost invariably funded entirely by the company, and, unlike all other retirement plans, they are intended to be invested primarily in employer securities. They also are unique in their ability to borrow money. ESOPs are not stock options (an entirely different way to share equity), nor can they be used to deliver stock just to selected employees, even on the basis of merit.

In 2008, there were about 10,000 ESOPs covering close to 11 million participants and holding about $700 billion in assets. ESOPs have thus become a significant part of the U.S. economy. They can be found in companies ranging in size from a handful of employees to hundreds of thousands. Their most common application, however, is in small to mid-sized privately held companies with at least 15 employees.

ESOPs have been granted a number of tax benefits that go beyond those normally available to retirement plans. Congress has seen the growth of broad ownership as good economic and social policy, a view that has been borne out by research showing that ESOPs generally enhance corporate performance and employee financial security, often substantially. ESOPs, of course, are not some magical elixir that need only be imbibed under an attorney's directions to produce magical effects. Successful ESOP companies work hard to integrate employees as owners, sharing information and work-level decision making with them in an effort to create a true ownership culture.

ESOP Applications

ESOPs are used for a wide variety of purposes:

- The most common application for an ESOP is to buy the shares of a departing owner of a closely held company. In C corporations, owners can defer taxes on the gain they make from the sale to an ESOP if the ESOP holds 30% or more of the company's stock and certain other requirements are met. Moreover, the purchase can be made in pretax corporate dollars. S corporations are often converted to C corporations before the sale, although with historically low capital gains rates, many S corporation owners choose to retain S status and go ahead and pay taxes now.

- ESOPs are also used to divest or acquire subsidiaries, buy back shares from the market (such as in the case of public companies seeking takeover defenses), or restructure existing benefit plans by replacing current benefit contributions with a leveraged ESOP (i.e., one that borrows money, as described later in this chapter).

- ESOPs can purchase newly issued shares in the company, with the borrowed funds being used to buy new productive capital or finance an acquisition. The company can, in effect, finance growth or acquisitions in pretax dollars while these same dollars create an employee benefit plan.

- The above uses generally involve borrowing money through the ESOP, but a company can simply contribute new shares of stock to an ESOP, or cash to buy existing shares, as a means to create an employee benefit plan. As more and more companies want to find ways to link employee and corporate interests, this is becoming a more popular application. In public companies especially, an ESOP contribution is often used as part or all of a match to employee deferrals to a 401(k) plan.

Different Tax Benefits for S and C Corporation ESOPs

In return for agreeing to fund the ESOP, the company gets a number of tax benefits, provided it follows the rules to assure employees are treated fairly. While some of these are the same for S and C corporation ESOPs, some differ. Table 1-1 provides details. The rest of the chapter explains each of these features and their requirements.

Financing an ESOP

A significant minority of ESOPs are funded by contributions of cash to the plan or, less often, by companies contributing newly issued shares. In new ESOPs, cash contributions are usually used to buy existing shares from an owner or owners. The company can also put cash in for some period of time, probably a few years, to build up a cash reserve to make a significant purchase of stock. As ESOPs mature, many companies make cash contributions to the ESOP, which the plan uses to create a reserve to buy shares back from employees. Each participant ends up with a stock account and a cash account within the plan. If the company simply contributes shares, it can take a tax deduction for them even though there is no immediate cash expense. Owners cannot contribute shares directly to the plan, however. In any direct contribution approach, each participant is credited with an allocation of his or her share of the contribution when it is made.

Even more rare is the use of existing employee money to help fund the ESOP. Most often, this comes from a voluntary transfer of 401(k) funds. Such transfers are subject to securities laws requirements and must meet strict ERISA rules for financial disclosure and prudence. Because compliance is very expensive, this approach is only used in large transactions needing an equity infusion.

The most common and powerful way to finance an ESOP, however, is to borrow money (a "leveraged ESOP"). The ESOP can borrow money from anyone, including commercial lenders, sellers of stock, or even the company itself. In this approach, the company sets up a trust, which then borrows money from a lender. The company repays the loan by making tax-deductible contributions to the trust that the trust gives to the lender. The trust must use the loan to acquire stock in the company. The company can use proceeds from the loan for any legitimate business purpose. Any loan to an ESOP must meet several requirements, however. It must have reasonable rates and terms, and it must be repaid only from employer contributions, dividends on

Table 1.1

Tax issue	S corporation ESOP	C corporation ESOP
Deferral of capital gains tax for sale to ESOP	No	Yes, if: 1. ESOP owns at least 30% after sale 2. Stock has been held three years before sale 3. Stock is reinvested in stocks and bonds of U.S. companies with not more than 25% of their income from passive investment 4. No direct relatives or more-than-25% shareholders receive an allocation of shares subject to the deferral from the sale in their ESOP accounts
Company does not pay federal or, usually, state income tax on share of profits attributable to the ESOP	Yes	Not available
Dividends paid on ESOP shares are deductible	No (S corporations do not pay dividends, and distributions are not deductible)	Yes, if used to repay an ESOP loan, passed through to employees, or voluntarily reinvested by employees in company stock
Contributions to the ESOP, either directly or to repay the ESOP debt, are deductible up to 25% of covered payroll (payroll of ESOP participants eligible to receive allocations and under $230,000 [as of 2008])	Both interest and principal payments count toward the 25% limit	Only payments toward principal must be counted toward 25% of covered payroll

Table 1.1

Forfeitures of unvested account balances from departed employees count toward limit on maximum annual additions to employee accounts (100% of pay or $46,000 [as of 2008]; includes all employer and employee contributions to retirement plans)	Yes	No
Distributions of account balances for departed participants can be delayed until after ESOP loan is repaid	No	Yes
In calculating the maximum amount that can go into a leveraged ESOP, employer contributions to qualified retirement plans do not count	No	Yes

shares in the plan, and earnings from other investments in the trust contributed by the employer. There is no limit on the term of an ESOP loan other than what lenders will accept (normally 5 to 10 years).

Shares in the plan are held in a suspense account. As the loan is repaid, these shares are released to the accounts of plan participants. The release must follow one of two formulas. The simpler of the two is the "principal-only" method, in which the percentage of shares released equals the percentage of principal paid, either that year or during whatever shorter repayment period is used. In such cases, however, the release may not be slower than what normal amortization schedules would provide for a 10-year loan with level payments of principal and interest. The principal-only method usually has the effect of releasing fewer shares to participants in the early years. Alternatively, the company can base its release on the total amount of principal and interest it pays each year. This method can be used for any loan, but it must be used for loans of more than 10 years. After employees leave the company or retire, the company distributes to them the stock purchased on their behalf, or its cash value. In practice, banks often insist on making the loan to the company instead of the trust, with the company re-loaning the proceeds to the ESOP.

In either case, it is important to remember that the value of the shares released each year is rarely the same as the amount contributed to repay the principal on the loan. If the price of the shares goes up, the amount released will be higher in dollar terms than the amount contributed; if it goes down, the dollar value of the amount released will be lower. The amount *contributed* to repay the principal on the loan is what counts for determining whether the company is within the limits for contributions allowed each year and for the purpose of calculating the tax deduction. The value of the shares released, however, is the amount used for accounting purposes on the income statement, where it counts as a compensation cost.

The loan to the company and the loan to the ESOP do not have to have the same terms. For instance, a company may want to extend the term of repayment of the "internal" loan so that contributions are made over a longer time. This might be done when to use the same term as the "outside" loan (from the lender to the company) would necessitate contributions to the ESOP above the contribution limits. In other cases, the contributions under a shorter term might be so high as to mean that employees in the early years of the ESOP would get dramatically more than employees who joined after the loan was repaid. The extension of an internal loan, however, must be in the interest of plan participants rather than primarily in the interest of the company or the sellers, and it must be on terms that are at least as good as an arm's-length equivalent.

Dividends (in C corporations) or distributions (in S corporations) can also be used to repay the debt. These are tax deductible in C corporations, but not in S (albeit this is not an issue for 100% S ESOPs that pay no taxes). The dividends or distributions release shares that have not yet been paid for into employee accounts, either on the basis on the pro-rata share of each employee's share account balance to the total shares in the plan or the company's normal compensation formula. For shares already in employee accounts, dividends or distributions would be used to pay for additional shares form the suspense account based on the employee's pro-rata share balance.

S corporations sometimes also use distributions paid to an ESOP to buy additional shares, even if these are not used to repay a loan. In an S corporation, distributions are normally made to owners so they can pay their share of income taxes on corporate profits. By law, any distributions must go pro-rata to all owners. So if the ESOP owns 30% of the stock, it must get 30% of the distributions. The ESOP can simply allocate this added cash to employee accounts (based on each employee's pro-rata share of the account balances) or use them to buy more shares. One disadvantage of this approach is that it means those employees with existing account balances get more and more shares, while newer employees get relatively less, or even nothing if no direct contributions to the ESOP are made. While some owners are happy with this approach, more often it causes problems in that there now are two classes of employees. In some cases, the approach can even cause companies to violate the "anti-abuse" rules described in detail later in this book. These problems can be avoided with good advice form counsel.

Limits on Contributions

In 2001, Congress made significant changes to contribution limits in all employee retirement plans. The new rules significantly raised these limits so that they are rarely an issue in ESOPs. Understanding two basic concepts will make these limits more intelligible. The first is "eligible pay." This refers to the compensation, either on an individual or aggregate basis, that can be counted in making contributions. Pay over certain amounts, the pay of "disqualified" individuals, and the pay of employees not yet participating in the plan are all examples of ineligible pay. The second is "annual additions." This refers to the amounts that are added to employee accounts in a year through corporate contributions and individual deferrals into retirement plans. Limits on annual additions to plans are covered by Section 415 of the Internal Revenue Code, so these limits are often called "Section 415 limits." Finally, a separate set of limits applies to how much a company can deduct when contributing to an ESOP or another retirement plans.

It is important to understand that for purposes of calculating the Section 415 limits in a leveraged ESOP, the amount that is defined as an "annual addition" to an employee's account is based on the amount the company contributed that year to repay that portion of the loan (either principal only or principal and interest, depending on the share release method used) attributable to the shares added to the employee's account. The actual value of the shares added to the employee's account, however, is usually different (e.g., if the per-share price is higher than at the time of purchase, the value of the shares added to the account will be higher than the amount defined as the "annual addition").

Generally, companies can deduct up to 25% of the total eligible payroll of plan participants to cover the principal portion of the loan and can deduct all of the interest they pay. Eligible pay includes all W-2 compensation plus employee deferrals into benefit plans, but only for employees actually in the plan. Pay over $230,000 per participant (as of 2008[1]) is not eligible. Company contributions to other defined contribution plans, such as stock bonus, 401(k), or profit sharing plans, must be counted in this 25% of pay calculation. On the other hand, "reasonable" dividends paid on shares acquired by a C corporation ESOP can be used to repay the loan and are not included in the 25% of pay calculations. Dividends in C corporations that are passed through

---

1.   This and other dollar limits designated here as being "as of 2008" are increased
     annually for inflation.

to employees or passed through and voluntarily reinvested in company stock are also deductible beyond the 25% limit. In a C corporation, if employees leave the company before they have a fully vested right to their ESOP shares, their forfeitures, which are allocated to everyone else, are not counted in the percentage limitations in leveraged ESOPs. If the ESOP does not borrow money, the annual contribution limit is also 25% of covered pay. Employer (but not employee), contributions to other plans reduce this amount.

In C corporations, there are separate 25% limits for (1) contributions to pay principal on an ESOP loan and (2) contributions to other defined contribution plans; thus, a company with a leveraged ESOP and a profit sharing plan, for example, has a 50% total limit (up to 25% for a leveraged ESOP plus up to 25% for other defined contribution plans such as the profit sharing plan). However, in S corporations, company contributions to both leveraged ESOPs and other defined contribution plans all fall under a single 25% of eligible pay calculation.

The above limits are for deductibility of aggregate corporate contributions; a separate set of limits applies to annual additions to individual employee accounts. First, no one ESOP participant can get more than 100% of pay in any year from company contributions to the ESOP, or more than $46,000 (as of 2008), whichever is less. In figuring payroll, pay over $230,000 per year (as of 2008) does not count toward total contribution limits.

Second, other qualified benefit plans must be taken into account when assessing this annual addition limit. This means that employee deferrals into 401(k) plans, as well as employer contributions to 401(k), stock bonus, or profit sharing plans, are added to the ESOP contribution and cannot exceed 100% of pay in any year.

Third, the interest on an ESOP loan is excludable from the 25% of pay individual limit in C corporations only if not more than one-third of the benefits are allocated to "highly compensated employees," as defined by the Internal Revenue Code (Section 414(q)). If the one-third rule is not met, forfeitures in C corporations are also counted in determining how much an employee is getting each year. If the company sponsoring the ESOP is an S corporation, interest is also not deductible, and forfeitures do count toward the 25% of pay limit.

How Shares Get to Employees

The rules for ESOPs are similar to the rules for other tax-qualified plans in terms of participation, allocation, vesting, and distribution, but several special considerations apply. All employees over age 21 who work for more than 1,000 hours in a plan year must be included, unless they are covered by a collective bargaining unit, are in a separate line of business with at least 50 employees not covered by the ESOP, or fall under one of several anti-discrimination exemptions not commonly used by ESOPs. If there is a union, the company must bargain in good faith with it over inclusion in the plan.

Shares are allocated to individual employee accounts based on relative compensation (generally, all W-2 compensation is counted), on a more level formula (such as per capita or seniority), or some combination thereof. The allocated shares are subject to vesting. Employees must be 100% vested after three years of service, or the company can use a graduated vesting schedule not slower than 20% after two years and 20% per year more until 100% is reached after six years. A faster vesting schedule applies where the ESOP contribution is used as a match to employee 401(k) deferrals. There, "cliff" vesting must be complete in three years, and graduated vesting must start after two years and be completed no later than after six years.

When employees reach age 55 and have 10 years of participation in the plan, the company must either give them the option of diversifying 25% of their account balances among at least three other investment alternatives or simply pay the amount out to the employees. At age 60, employees can have 50% diversified or distributed to them.

When employees retire, die, or are disabled, the company must distribute their vested shares to them or their heirs not later than the last day of the plan year following the year of the departure. For employees leaving before reaching retirement age, distribution must begin not later than the last day of the sixth plan year following the year of separation from service. C corporations can delay this distribution to terminated employees (other than for death, retirement, or disability) until after the ESOP loan is repaid. Payments can be in substantially equal installments out of the trust over five years, or in a lump sum. In the installment method, a company normally pays out a portion of the stock from the trust each year. The value of that stock may go up or down over that time, of course. In a lump-sum distribution, the company buys the shares at their current value, but it can make the purchase in installments over five years, as long as it provides adequate security and reasonable interest. ESOP shares must be valued at least annually by an independent outside appraiser unless the shares are publicly traded.

Closely held companies and some thinly traded public companies must repurchase the shares from departing employees at their fair market value, as determined by an independent appraiser. This "put option" can be exercised by the employee in one of two 60-day periods, one starting when the employee receives the distribution and the second period one year after that. The employee can choose which one to use. This obligation should be considered at the outset of the ESOP and factored into the company's ability to repay the loan.

Voting Rules

Voting is one of the most controversial and least understood of ESOP issues. The trustee of the ESOP actually votes the ESOP shares. The question is, "Who directs the trustee?" The trustee can make the decision independently, although that is very rare. Alternatively, management or the ESOP administrative committee can direct the trustee, or the trustee can follow employee directions.

In private companies, employees must be able to direct the trustee as to the voting of shares *allocated* to their accounts on several key issues, including closing, sale, liquidation, recapitalization, and other issues having to do with the basic structure of the company. They do not, however, have to be able to vote for the board of directors or on other typical corporate governance issues, although companies can voluntarily provide these rights. Instead, the plan trustee votes the shares, usually at the direction of management. In public companies, employees must be able to vote on all issues.

Voting rights are more complicated than they seem. First, voting is not the same as tendering shares. So while employees may be required to be able to vote on all issues, they may have no say about whether shares are tendered. In public companies, this is a major issue. Almost all public companies now write their plans to give employees the right to direct the tendering, as well as voting, of their shares, for reasons to be explained below.

Second, employers are not required to allow employees to vote on unallocated shares. In a leveraged ESOP, this means that for the first several years of the loan, the trustee can vote the majority of the shares, if that is what the company wants to do. The company could provide that unallocated shares, as well as any allocated shares for which the trustee has not received instructions, should be voted or tendered in proportion to the allocated shares for which directions were received.

What this all means is that for almost all ESOP companies, governance is not really an issue unless they want it to be. If companies want employees to have only the most limited role in corporate governance, they can; if they want to go beyond this, they can as well. In practice, companies that do provide employees with a substantial governance role find that it does not result in dramatic changes in the way the company is run.

Valuation

In closely held companies and some thinly traded public companies, every ESOP transaction must be based on a current appraisal by an independent, outside valuation expert. The valuation process assesses how much a willing buyer would pay a willing seller for the business. This calculation is performed by looking at, among other things, various ratios, such as the price-to-earnings ratio; at discounted future cash flow and earnings; at asset value; and at the market value of comparable companies. It is then adjusted to reflect whether the sale is for control (owning a controlling interest in a business is worth more than owning a minority interest, even on a per-share basis) and marketability (shares of public companies are worth more than shares of closely held companies because public company shares are easier to buy and sell). ESOP company shares have better marketability than those of non-ESOP companies, however, because the ESOP provides a market, albeit not as active a one as a stock exchange. The appraisal must be performed by an independent, outside appraiser (one without another business relationship with the company) working for the ESOP trust, not the company. The appraiser determines the maximum the ESOP can pay; in some cases, the ESOP trustee may argue that the price should or could be lower and negotiate for that better price.

Fiduciary Issues

Like other tax-qualified retirement plans, an ESOP must have a trustee who makes decisions concerning plan assets. The most important decisions concern voting ESOP shares, deciding whether the price the ESOP is paying is not more than fair market value, deciding whether to tender shares in an acquisition offer or merger, and making sure the plan's administration follows plan and statutory rules. The trustee may take directions from another party, such as the board, employees (when companies pass through voting or tendering decisions), or management, however. The individual or entity making decisions is always considered the plan fiduciary and is legally responsible for how those decisions are made. If the trustee is directed by a third party acting as fiduciary, then the trustee has less of a fiduciary responsibility but still must make sure that decisions are in compliance with the law and plan documents. Fiduciaries should be indemnified by the company and insured, as they are personally responsible in the case of adverse judgments. In evaluating whether a fiduciary performed his or her duties, courts look to the process more than the results. At the time a decision is made, fiduciaries should, at the least:

- Rely on qualified, independent advice from experienced ESOP advisors;

- Conduct an independent evaluation of the issue and make a prudent decision based on the best interests of plan participants as participants in a benefit plan, rather than solely as employees of the company;

- Not be in a conflict-of-interest situation, such as a seller would be in judging whether the ESOP is paying a fair price for his or her stock; and

- Be knowledgeable about the law and current best practices.

Most larger companies hire independent trustees to act as fiduciaries. These trustees provide a kind of insurance, because courts tend to ascribe more credibility to the independence and judgment of a fiduciary who is an experienced outside expert. Outside trustees are costly, however, so most smaller companies use corporate officers (other than the sellers) or committees of employees, sometimes including nonmanagement employees.

Tax Benefits to the Selling Shareholder

One of the major benefits of an ESOP for a closely held company is Section 1042 of the Internal Revenue Code. Under it, a seller to an ESOP may be able to qualify for a deferral of taxation on the gain made from the sale. Several requirements apply, the most significant of which are:

1. The seller must have held the stock for three years before the sale.

2. The stock must not have been acquired through options or other employee benefit plans.

3. The ESOP must own 30% or more of the value of the shares in the company and must continue to hold this amount for three years unless the company is sold. Shares repurchased by the company from departing employees do not count. Stock sold in a transaction that brings the ESOP to 30% of the total shares qualifies for the deferral treatment.

4. Shares qualifying for the deferral cannot be allocated to accounts of children, brothers or sisters, spouses, or parents of the selling shareholder(s), or to other 25% shareholders.

5. The company must be a C corporation.

If these rules are met, the sellers can take the proceeds from the sale and reinvest them in "qualified replacement property" between 3 months before and 12 months after the sale and defer any capital gains taxes until these new investments are sold. Qualified replacement property is defined essentially as stocks, bonds, warrants, or debentures of domestic corporations receiving not more than 25% of their income from passive investment. Mutual funds and real estate trusts do not qualify. If the replacement property is held until death, they are subject to a step-up in basis, so capital gains taxes are never due.

Increasingly, lenders are asking for the replacement property as part or all of the collateral for an ESOP loan. This strategy may be beneficial to sellers selling only part of their holdings because it frees the corporation to use its assets for other borrowing and could enhance the future value of the company.

It is also important to note that people taking advantage of the 1042 treatment cannot have stock reallocated to their accounts from these sales if they remain employees. More-than-25% shareholders and close relatives of the seller also cannot receive allocations from these sales.

As noted earlier, sellers in S corporations cannot receive this tax benefit. Many S corporations convert to C status before selling to the ESOP, then may reconvert to S status after the loan is rapid (conversion cannot occur sooner than five years after leaving S status, however). During the period when the acquisition loan is being repaid, deductions often eliminate much or even all of the income tax obligation, so S status is less important. Other owners, however, choose to retain S status. They may have relatives they want to be in the plans, or they may want to stay in the plan themselves if they are still working. There may also be more-than-25% shareholders who cannot receive 1042 treatment. In addition, with federal capital gains tax rates at 15%, many owners decide it is better to pay tax at this low rate now, and be able to invest in whatever they want, then defer tax into a more limited set of investments and pay later when the rate may be higher.

Other reasons that may make S-to-C conversion unwise include:

- *There are large amounts of undistributed earnings.* When the conversion to a C corporation takes place, any earnings that have not yet been contributed to the owners must be distributed in one year or they are taxable to the owners (meaning they will be taxed twice, since the owners have already paid tax on them before). If the company does not have the cash to do this, it could borrow money, but the ESOP may itself require too much cash to make this payout practical.

- *Remaining owners plan to sell the company in an asset sale some time after the ESOP is implemented.* In an S corporation, the sale of the company's assets trigger only a single tax at the individual level; in a C corporation, the sale would be taxed at both the corporate and individual level, as income to the company and as capital gains to the individuals. The amount of the corporate tax would depend in part on the depreciation taken on the assets.

- *The S corporation is creating losses the owners want flowed through to them.* In some situations, a company may be making heavy investments, often in real property or other hard assets, that create paper losses. These losses can be flowed through to the owners, who can deduct them at a marginally higher rate than can the company. In some scenarios, this may be desirable.

- *The seller's basis is already very high* because of taxes paid on previously undistributed earnings. In this case, the Section 1042 "rollover" provision may not make much difference.

Financial Issues for Employees

When an employee receives a distribution from the plan, it is taxable unless rolled over into an IRA or other qualified plan. Otherwise, the amounts contributed by the employer are taxable as ordinary income, while any appreciation on the shares is taxable as capital gains. In addition, if the employee receives the distribution before normal retirement age and does not roll over the funds, a 10% excise tax is added.

While the stock is in the plan, however, it is not taxable to employees. It is rare, moreover, for employees to give up wages to participate in an ESOP or to purchase stock directly through a plan (this raises difficult securities law issues for closely held companies). Most ESOPs either are in addition to existing benefit plans or replace other defined contribution plans, usually at a higher level of pay.

Determining ESOP Feasibility

Several factors are involved in determining whether a company is a good ESOP candidate:

- *Is the cost reasonable?* ESOPs typically cost $30,000 to $40,000 and up, depending on complexity and the size of the transaction. This is usually much cheaper than other ways to sell a business, but more expensive than other benefit plans.

- *Is the payroll large enough?* Limitations on how much can be contributed to a plan may make it impractical to use to buy out a major owner or finance a large transaction. For instance, a $5 million purchase would not be feasible if the company has $500,000 of eligible payroll, because annual contributions could be no larger than $125,000 per year, not enough to repay a loan for that amount. Flexibility in the term of the ESOP loan, the ability to use dividends that do not count toward the limits (in C corporations), and the generous contribution limits available nowadays, however, make this problem relatively rare.

- *Can the company afford the contributions?* Many ESOPs are used to buy existing shares, a nonproductive expense. Companies need to assess whether they have the available earnings for this.

- *Is management comfortable with the idea of employees as owners?* While employees do not have to run the company, they will want more information and more say. Unless they are treated this way, research shows, they are likely to be demotivated by ownership.

The Repurchase Obligation

One of the major issues ESOPs must face is the obligation that closely held companies sponsoring them provide for the repurchase of shares of departing employees. The legal obligation rests with the company, although it can fund this by making tax-deductible contributions to the ESOP, which the ESOP uses to repurchase the shares. Most companies either do this or buy the shares back themselves and then recontribute them to the ESOP (and take a tax deduction for that). Either way, shares continue to circulate in the plan, providing stock for new employees. Some companies, however, buy back the shares and retire them or have other people buy them (a manager, for instance).

The repurchase obligation may seem like a reason not to do an ESOP ("You mean we have to buy back the shares continually?" people often ask). In fact, all closely held companies have a 100% repurchase obligation at all times. An ESOP simply puts it on a schedule and allows the company to do it in pretax dollars. Nonetheless, repurchase can be a major problem if companies do not anticipate and plan for it. A careful repurchase study should be done periodically to help manage this process.

Steps to Setting Up an ESOP

If you have decided an ESOP is worth investigating, there are several steps to take to implement a plan. At each point, you may decide that you have gone far enough and an ESOP is not right for you.

1. Determine Whether Other Owners Are Amenable

This may seem like an obvious issue, but sometimes people take several of the steps listed below before finding out whether the existing owners are willing to sell. Employees should not start organizing a buyout unless they have some reason to think the parent firm is willing to sell (it may not be, for instance, if its goal is to reduce total output of a product it makes at other locations). Or there may be other owners of a private company who will never agree to an ESOP, even if it seems appealing to the principal owners. They could cause a good deal of trouble down the road.

2. Conduct a Feasibility Study

This may be a full-blown analysis by an outside consultant, replete with market surveys, management interviews, and detailed financial projections, or it may simply be a careful business plan performed in-house. Generally, full-scale feasibility studies are needed only where there is some doubt about the ESOP's ability to repay the loan. Any analysis, however, must look at several items. First, it must assess just how much extra cash flow the company has available to devote to the ESOP, and whether this is adequate for the purposes for which the ESOP is intended. Second, it must determine whether the company has adequate payroll for ESOP participants to make the ESOP contributions deductible. Remember to include the effect of other benefit plans that will be maintained in these calculations. Third, estimates must be made of the repurchase obligation (if the company is closely held) and thought given to how the company will handle it.

3. Conduct a Valuation

The feasibility study will rely on rough estimates of the value of the stock for the purpose of calculating the adequacy of cash and payroll. In public companies, of course, these estimates will be fairly accurate because they can be based on past price performance. In private companies, they will be more speculative. The next step for private companies (and some public companies as well) is a valuation. A company may want to have a preliminary valuation done first to see if the range of values produced is acceptable. A full valuation would follow if it is. Doing a valuation before implementing a plan is critical. If the value is too low, sellers may not be willing to sell. Or the price of the shares may be too high for the company to afford. The valuation consultant will look at a variety of factors, including cash flow, profits, market conditions, assets, comparable company values, goodwill, and overall economic factors. A discount on value may be taken if the ESOP is buying less than 5% of the shares.

4. Hire an ESOP Attorney

If the first three steps prove positive, the plan can now be drafted and submitted to the IRS. You should carefully evaluate your options and tell your attorney just how you want the ESOP to be set up. This could save you a considerable amount of money in consultation time. The IRS may take many months to issue you a "letter of determination" on your plan, but you can go ahead and start making contributions before then. If the IRS rules unfavorably, which rarely happens, normally you just need to amend your plan.

5. Obtain Funding for the Plan

We have previously discussed the variety of methods available for funding. Keep in mind that many plans combine approaches. Of particular note is the increase in seller-financed ESOPs. Although banks have generally been positive about ESOP lending, more sellers are choosing to take a note from the ESOP instead. This avoids the costs and potential delays of obtaining a bank loan. The note must be on terms at least as favorable as an arms-length equivalent transaction. The loan may be made directly to the ESOP or to the company, which reloans it to the ESOP. This allows the company to repay the loan to the seller on different terms than those with which the ESOP repays its loan to the company. One possible downside to seller financing is that the seller will receive a stream of payments over the years; yet, if the seller wishes to take advantage of the Section 1042 tax deferral, the seller must buy all the securities within a year after the ESOP transaction, i.e., before the seller has received most of the money (assuming a multi-year loan).[2] Seller-financed transactions in C corporations that are designed to take advantage of the Section 1042 tax deferral are possible but require an additional step beyond the scope of this chapter (see our book *Selling to an ESOP* for details).

6. Establish a Process for Operating the Plan

A trustee must be chosen to oversee the plan. In most private companies, this will be someone from inside the firm, but some private and most public companies hire outside trustees. An ESOP committee will direct the trustee. In most companies, this is made up of management people, but many ESOP firms allow at least some nonmanagement representation. Finally, and most important, a process must be established to communicate to employees how the plan works and to get them more involved as owners. These issues are also addressed in more detail later in this book.

---

2. The qualified replacement property bought for the Section 1042 tax deferral need not be bought with the actual proceeds of the transaction, but many sellers do not have an equivalent amount of cash on hand.

CHAPTER TWO

Legal Considerations for S Corporation ESOPs

David Ackerman

Acorporation that sponsors an employee stock ownership plan (an ESOP) can obtain extraordinary tax savings by making the election to be treated as an "S corporation" for federal income tax purposes.[1] An S corporation generally is not subject to federal income tax.[2] Instead, the shareholders of the corporation are subject to tax on the corporation's earnings, whether they are distributed to them as dividends or retained in the corporation.[3] An important tax advantage of this treatment is that only one tax is imposed on the earnings of an S corporation. Regular or "C" corporations are subject to a "double tax"—once at the corporate level[4] and again at the shareholder level when the after-tax corporate earnings are distributed to the shareholders.[5]

This chapter summarizes the rules relating to S corporation ESOPs, as set forth in the Internal Revenue Code of 1986 (the "Code"). This chapter also provides a brief analysis of situations where either an ESOP may be appropriate for an S corporation or where an existing ESOP company might benefit from making the S election. Finally, to provide a context for this discussion, this chapter concludes with a brief summary of how S corporations are taxed and the benefits of the S election.

---

1. Internal Revenue Code ("Code") § 1361(c)(6).

2. Code § 1363(a).

3. Code § 1366(a).

4. Code § 11.

5. Code § 301. The impact of the double tax has been reduced by the Jobs and Growth Tax Relief Reconciliation Act of 2003, which reduced the maximum rate of tax on dividends to 15%.

The Applicable Tax Laws

Authorization of S Corporation ESOPs

To be eligible to make the S election, a corporation may not have more than 100 shareholders, and the corporation may have only one class of stock outstanding.[6] In addition, all shareholders must be U.S. citizens or U.S. residents, and they must be natural persons, estates, or certain types of trusts (including employee benefit trusts).[7] An employee benefit plan trust is treated as a single shareholder of an S corporation.[8] This is of critical importance because of the 100-shareholder limit for S corporations. If each participant in an employee benefit plan were treated as a shareholder of the plan sponsor, then many ESOP companies would be rendered ineligible to make the S election by reason of the 100-shareholder limit.

Exemption from Unrelated Business Income Tax

Shares of an S corporation held by an employee benefit trust generally are treated as an interest in an "unrelated trade or business," with the result that the trust's share of the S corporation's income generally is taken into account in computing the trust's unrelated business income tax (UBIT).[9] In addition, any gain or loss realized by an employee benefit trust in connection with the disposition of employer securities generally must be taken into account for this purpose.[10] However, there is a special exemption from the application of the unrelated business income tax to ESOPs that hold stock of an S corporation.[11]

---

6.   Code § 1361(b)(1)(A), (D).

7.   Code § 1361(b) (1)(B). For a more detailed discussion of the S corporation eligibility requirements, see discussion below at footnotes 117–26.

8.   S. Rep. No.105-35, 105th Cong., 1st Sess. (1997).

9.   Code § 512(e).

10. Code § 512(e)(1)(B).

11. Code § 512(e)(3).

Special Distribution Rules

Generally, participants in an ESOP are entitled to demand that their benefits be distributed to them in the form of stock of the sponsoring employer.[12] However, there is an exception to this rule pursuant to which an S corporation that sponsors an ESOP may require the participants in the plan to take their benefits in the form of cash.[13] This exception enables S corporations that sponsor ESOPs to avoid involuntary terminations of the S election, which otherwise could arise in either of two ways. First, a participant might request that the shares of employer stock allocated to his or her account be rolled over to an individual retirement arrangement (IRA). An IRA is not eligible to own shares of an S corporation.[14] Second, over time, if enough participants in the plan elect to take their benefits in the form of employer shares, the 100-shareholder limit might be exceeded. These problems can be avoided by requiring the participants in the ESOP to take their benefits in the form of cash.[15]

Inapplicability of Certain C Corporation Tax Incentives

Some of the tax incentives that have been provided for C corporations to adopt ESOPs do not apply to S corporations:

---

12. Code § 409(h)(1)(A). This right can be denied to ESOP participants if the articles of incorporation or bylaws of the ESOP company restrict the ownership of substantially all outstanding employer securities to employees or to a qualified retirement plan. Code § 409(h)(2).

13. Code § 409(h)(2).

14. Code § 1361(b)(1)(B). However, in PLR 200122034 (Feb. 28, 2001), the Internal Revenue Service (the "IRS") ruled that momentary ownership of S corporation stock by an IRA would not result in an involuntary termination of the corporation's S election where the stock had been received in a direct transfer from an ESOP and was subject to the requirement that it be immediately sold back to the sponsor of the ESOP. In Revenue Procedure 2004-14, the IRS held that it was permissible for the ESOP trust, as well as for the plan sponsor, to buy the shares.

15. Code § 409(h)(2).

- Upon the sale of an individual shareholder's stock to an S corporation ESOP, he or she will not qualify for the tax-deferred "rollover" that is available to individual shareholders of a C corporation;[16]

- The increased limits for tax deductions for contributions to a leveraged ESOP, when used to pay interest on an exempt loan to the plan, are not available for S corporations;[17] and

- S corporations are not entitled to deduct cash dividends paid on stock held by an ESOP that are used to pay principal or interest on a loan used to acquire the stock or that are passed through to plan participants.[18]

No Section 1042 Tax-Deferred Sales

A tax incentive that has spurred great interest in ESOPs for closely held companies is the opportunity provided under Section 1042 of the Code for a tax-free "rollover" of the proceeds of a sale of stock by a shareholder to an ESOP if the proceeds are reinvested in securities of other corporations.[19] However, this special tax treatment is available only with sales of stock of closely held C corporations.[20]

Limit on Contributions

The maximum amount that a corporation may deduct for contributions to an ESOP generally is 25% of the compensation paid to all employees participating in the plan for the taxable year.[21] However, increased limits for employer contributions are available for amounts allocated to repay an ESOP loan incurred to finance the purchase of employer stock. Contributions by a C corporation used to pay interest on this kind of a loan are fully deductible in addition to contributions used to pay the principal amount of an ESOP loan, which are deduct-

---

16. Code § 1042(c)(1)(A).
17. Code § 404(a)(9)(c).
18. Code § 404(k)(1).
19. Code § 1042(a).
20. Code § 1042(c)(1)(A).
21. Code § 404(a)(3)(A).

ible up to 25% of the compensation of the participating employees.[22] However, contributions by an S corporation used to pay interest on an ESOP loan will count against the 25% limit.[23]

No Deduction for Dividends

Dividends paid on shares held by a C corporation ESOP may be deducted under the following circumstances: (1) if they are paid in cash to plan participants; (2) if they are paid to the plan and passed through to the participants within 90 days after the end of the plan year; (3) if they are used to repay a loan incurred to purchase the company stock on which the dividends are paid; or (4) if they are paid to the plan and, at the election of the plan participants, are reinvested in employer securities.[24] However, this deduction for dividends on stock held by an ESOP is not available for S corporations.[25] Where an S corporation ESOP owns all of the outstanding shares of the corporation, the fact that dividends are not deductible will not have any effect because the corporation's income will not be subject to tax, either at the corporate or at the shareholder level.[26] However, in the situation where an ESOP owns less than all of the outstanding shares of the plan sponsor, the failure of Congress to extend the dividends-paid deduction to S corporation ESOPs may result in greater taxable income for the other shareholders than would be the case with a C corporation declaring the same amount of dividends.

Unresolved Issues

Distributions of S Corporation Earnings to Plan Participants

Excise Tax on Premature Distributions. One area of ambiguity regarding the rules for S corporation ESOPs relates to how distributions of S

---

22. Code § 404(a)(9). This amount is deductible *in addition to* contributions used for other purposes, which are deductible up to 25% of covered compensation. See PLR 200732028.
23. Code § 404(a)(9)(C).
24. Code § 404(k).
25. Code § 404(k)(1).
26. Code §§ 1363(a) and 501(a).

corporation earnings to ESOP participants should be treated. Distributions received from a tax-qualified plan by a participant before he or
she has attained age 59½ are subject to a 10% excise tax.[27] This tax does
not apply to "dividends" on stock of a C corporation as described in
Section 404(k) of the Code.[28] Section 404(k) of the Code provides, as
a general rule, that in the case of a C corporation, there will be allowed
as a deduction the amount of any dividend paid on shares held by an
ESOP if the dividend is paid in cash to the participants in the plan, is
used to make payments on an ESOP loan, or is reinvested in employer
securities.[29] Because distributions by S corporations technically do not
constitute "dividends" within the meaning of the Code,[30] the question
arises whether the pass-through of S corporation earnings to ESOP plan
participants should be treated in the same manner as dividends declared

---

27. Code § 72(t).

28. Code § 72(t)(2)(A)(vi).

29. Code § 404(k)(2).

30. The term "dividend" is defined in Section 316 of the Code to mean any
    distribution of property made by a corporation to its shareholders out of its
    current or accumulated "earnings and profits." In the case of a C corpora-
    tion, a distribution that is a dividend is included in the gross income of the
    shareholders to whom the dividend is paid. Code § 301(c). Different rules are
    provided for distributions of property made by S corporations with respect to
    their stock. If an S corporation has no earnings and profits from years during
    which it was a C corporation, distributions then generally will be tax-free to
    the extent of the shareholders' bases in their stock. Code § 1368(b). An S
    corporation shareholder will be subject to tax on any distribution to the extent
    that it exceeds his or her stock basis. Code § 1368(b)(2). If a C corporation
    converts to S corporation status at a time when it has accumulated earnings
    and profits, then distributions will remain tax-free up to the amount of the
    corporation's "accumulated adjustments account," which is an account
    consisting of the corporation's net undistributed income accumulated after
    1982. Code § 1368(c). If a distribution exceeds the accumulated adjust-
    ments account, the excess amount is treated as a dividend to the extent of
    the corporation's accumulated earnings and profits. Code § 1368(c)(2). In
    other words, a distribution by an S corporation with respect to its stock is not
    a "dividend" for tax purposes unless the amount of the distribution exceeds
    the corporation's accumulated adjustments account and the corporation has
    accumulated earnings and profits.

by a C corporation that are passed through to ESOP participants, or whether the excise tax on premature distributions should apply.

Small Cash-Outs. A related issue is whether the consent of the ESOP participants must be obtained before distributions from an S corporation to an ESOP may be passed through to the participants. No accrued benefit under an employee benefit plan with a present value in excess of $1,000 may be immediately distributed to a participant in a tax-qualified employee benefit plan without his or her consent.[31] This provision does not apply to a distribution of dividends from an ESOP to which Section 404(k) of the Code applies.[32] Because the exception applies only to "dividends," it could be argued that the general rule requiring employee consent to distributions applies to all distributions from an S corporation ESOP, including distributions of the S corporation's earnings. It is not clear whether Congress intended that different rules would apply with regard to distributions of C corporation and S corporation earnings.

IRA Rollovers

Another issue relating to distributions of S corporation earnings to ESOP participants is whether these distributions are eligible for a tax-free rollover into an individual retirement arrangement (an "IRA") or into another tax-qualified plan. The regulations exclude from the definition of an "eligible rollover distribution" dividends paid on employer securities as described in Section 404(k) of the Code.[33] Before the enactment of the American Jobs Creation Act of 2004, the IRS had taken the position that distributions by an S corporation on stock that is not pledged as collateral to secure an ESOP loan could not be used to pay off that loan because those distributions are not "dividends" within the meaning of Section 404(k) of the Code.[34] By this reasoning,

---

31. Code § 411(a)(11).

32. Code § 404(k)(1).

33. Treas. Regs. § 1.402(c)-2, Q&A 4(e).

34. PLR 199938052 (July 2, 1999). The American Jobs Creation Act of 2004 contained a provision authorizing the use by an ESOP of distributions on S

it would seem to follow that S corporation distributions should not be treated as dividends that are not eligible for a tax-free rollover.[35]

Delayed Distribution of Leveraged Shares

Section 409(o)(1)(B) of the Code generally permits an ESOP to defer the commencement of distributions of shares acquired with a "loan described in Section 404(a)(9)" until the complete repayment of that loan. Section 404(a)(9) provides that, notwithstanding the general limitations on the amounts that may be contributed to defined contribution pension plans, contributions made to an ESOP and applied by the plan to the repayment of the principal of a loan incurred for the purpose of acquiring qualifying employer securities are deductible up to 25% of the compensation otherwise paid or accrued during the taxable year to the employees under the ESOP.[36] It is unclear whether a loan to an S corporation ESOP is "described in Section 404(a)(9)" for this purpose, because Section 404(a)(9)(c) provides that "[t]his paragraph shall not apply to an S corporation." IRS representatives have informally indicated that Section 409(o)(1)(B) is not applicable to an S corporation ESOP, but the author is aware that a number of favorable determination letters have been issued for S corporation ESOPs incorporating the deferral of distributions permitted by this section of the Code.

---

corporation stock that has not been pledged as collateral to secure an ESOP loan to pay off that loan. P.L. 108-357, 118 Stat. 1418, §240(a).

35. The author is aware that representatives of the national office of the IRS have informally expressed the view that distributions of S corporation earnings are not "dividends" within the meaning of Section 316 of the Code and that, therefore: (1) S corporation distributions are subject to the 10% excise tax on premature distributions if they are passed through to participants in an ESOP; (2) the consent of an ESOP participant must be obtained before a distribution from an S corporation to an ESOP may be passed through to him or her; and (iii) S corporation distributions are eligible for a tax-free rollover into an IRA.

36. Code § 404(a)(9)(C).

Planning Opportunities

Income Tax Deferral

Significant tax savings opportunities are available for ESOP companies that make the S election. This can be illustrated most dramatically by considering a corporation in which an ESOP owns all of the stock. If that corporation makes the S election, there will be <u>no current federal tax on its annual income</u>. The corporation will not be subject to tax under the general S corporation rules,[37] and although the income will be passed through to its sole shareholder (the ESOP), no shareholder-level tax will be imposed because the ESOP is a tax-exempt entity.[38] <u>In effect, the income tax will be deferred until the participants in the ESOP receive their benefits</u> (which will most likely be much larger than they would have been if the ESOP trust had been taxed on its share of the S corporation earnings). It should also be noted that participants may further defer their tax liability by rolling their benefits over into IRAs.[39] However, as discussed below, certain additional taxes are imposed on S corporations and participants in S corporation ESOPs where the benefits under an ESOP are allocated primarily to a small group of employees or where the corporation has issued large and concentrated amounts of synthetic equity.

100% ESOP

Where an ESOP company has shareholders in addition to the ESOP, tax savings still will be available by making the S election, but <u>the S election may not have a positive impact on the corporation's cash flow</u>. This is because, in most cases, <u>S corporation shareholders must withdraw sufficient funds to cover payment of their taxes on the corporation's income</u>. If tax distributions are required to be made to the shareholders other than the ESOP, an equivalent distribution also will have to be made to the ESOP, even though it will incur no tax liability, because otherwise the economic rights associated with the ESOP's shares will be different from those associated with the other shares. This, of course, would violate the one-class-of-stock rule for S

---

37. Code § 1363(a).

38. Code §§ 401(a), 501(a), and 512(e)(3).

39. Code § 402(c).

corporations and result in termination of the S election.[40] The potential impact of the S election on an ESOP company's cash flow can be illustrated by the following example:

Example 1. Assume that an S corporation sponsors an ESOP that owns 30% of its outstanding shares and that its taxable income for 2008 is $1 million. There will be allocated to the shareholders other than the ESOP $700,000 of the corporation's income, upon which they will incur a federal tax liability of approximately $245,000.[41] If the corporation distributes $245,000 to the other shareholders, it will be required to distribute an equivalent amount, or $105,000, to the ESOP. After the distributions, the S corporation will have retained earnings of $650,000. If the corporation were a C corporation, its corporate tax liability would be $350,000,[42] and the corporation would be able to retain $650,000 after taxes (assuming no dividends are declared), or as much as in the S corporation case.

This example illustrates that the S election may not be advantageous for a rapidly growing ESOP company that needs to retain earnings to fund future expansion (unless all of the company's shares are held by the ESOP). On the other hand, the S election still might be advantageous under various other circumstances. For example, the S election would be advantageous where the corporation could declare dividends in an amount in excess of the shareholders' tax liability because it did not need to retain most of its earnings. The S election also would be advantageous if the cash distributed to the ESOP could be used to fund other corporate obligations. This might be the case where the cash distributed to the ESOP could be used to fund the corporation's repurchase obligation.[43] The S election also might be advantageous

---

40. Code § 1361(b)(1)(D).

41. This calculation assumes that the shareholders are in the maximum individual tax bracket of 35%. Code § 1.

42. This calculation assumes that the corporation is subject to tax at the rate of 35% of its taxable income. Code § 11(b).

43. Until 2004, there was some ambiguity regarding whether S corporation distributions on allocated ESOP shares could be used to pay down an ESOP loan. As discussed at footnote 34, the IRS had taken the position that this could not be done, PLR 199938052 (July 2, 1999), but the Code was amended in 2004 to specifically allow S corporation distributions to be so used. American Jobs Creation of 2004, P.L. 108-357, 118 Stat. 1418, §240(a).

where the cash distributed to the ESOP could be used to buy more shares from the plan sponsor, which then could use the sale proceeds to provide funds for other business needs. This would require the approval of the ESOP trustee or other fiduciary, who would have to determine that the proposed use of the cash is in the best interest of the participants in the plan.[44]

Another situation where the S election would be advantageous would be where the individual shareholders are willing to pay the tax on their share of the corporation's income out of their own personal funds. This might be feasible in a situation where the ESOP owns most, but not all, of the outstanding shares. If the individual shareholders have substantial personal wealth in addition to their company stock, or if they are employed by the corporation and their compensation can be increased to an amount where they are willing to pay the tax on their share of the S corporation's earnings out of their own funds, it may be possible for the corporation to avoid the payment of dividends.

Should ESOP Companies Make the S Election?

Income Tax Deferral

The question whether existing ESOP companies should make the S election can be determined only on a case-by-case basis, depending on each company's particular facts and circumstances. In some cases, the opportunity for the tax deferral described above will be appealing. However, because most individual S corporation shareholders require distributions to cover the taxes on their share of the corporation's income, the ESOP companies that will derive a significant benefit from the tax-deferral opportunity may be limited to those companies where the ESOP owns all or substantially all of the outstanding shares.

Tax-Deferred Sales to ESOPs

The failure of Congress to extend to S corporations all of the ESOP tax incentives that are available to C corporations also will limit the number of ESOP companies that make the S election. Most importantly,

---

44. ERISA § 404(a)(1)(A).

where individual shareholders of an ESOP company are planning to arrange tax-deferred sales of some or all of their shares to the ESOP in the future, the S election will be unattractive. However, it may be possible for a shareholder who desires to arrange for a tax-deferred sale to an ESOP to obtain the best of both worlds by arranging for the sale to close in a year when the plan sponsor is a C corporation and for the S election to be made effective for a later year. A problem will remain for business owners who desire to arrange for two or three-stage ESOP buyouts. If an S election is made after the first ESOP sale, subsequent sales of stock to the ESOP will not qualify for the tax deferral unless the S election is first terminated. Once an S election is terminated, it cannot be reinstated for five years.[45]

In some cases, shareholders of S corporations have built up significant tax bases in the shares of their S corporations, and sales of their shares to an ESOP might be attractive even without the opportunity for a deferral of the capital gains tax. An S corporation shareholder's basis in his or her shares is increased by his or her share of the corporation's income and is reduced by distributions.[46] To the extent that an S corporation has retained earnings, the shareholders will have increased tax bases in their shares. Another situation in which an S corporation shareholder may have a high stock basis is where the stock has recently been inherited. In that case, the shareholder's basis is equal to the fair market value as of the date of the decedent's death.[47] Where an S corporation shareholder has a high basis in his or her shares, the shares can be sold at a reduced capital gain. The less the amount of the gain, the less important the tax-deferral election becomes. The importance of the tax-deferral election also is lessened when capital-gains tax rates are relatively low, as has been the case during the first decade of the 21st century.

---

45. Code § 1362(g). The IRS has stated that it will not exercise its authority to waive this rule when a 50% ownership change has occurred if that ownership change arises in connection with a sale of stock to an ESOP which qualifies for nonrecognition of gain under Section 1042 of the Code. PLR 199952072 (Sept. 27, 1999).

46. Code § 1367(a).

47. Code § 1014.

Limits on Plan Contributions

The attractiveness of the S election for an ESOP company also may be reduced by the fact that the limit on the amount that can be contributed to a leveraged ESOP by an S corporation is lower than the amount that can be contributed by a C corporation. The limit on tax-deductible contributions is 25% of covered compensation, but in the case of an S corporation, contributions applied to pay interest on an ESOP loan count against the limit,[48] while contributions to an ESOP by a C corporation for this purpose do not count against the limit.[49] However, in most cases where the annual payments due under the ESOP loan exceed the maximum amount that can be contributed to the ESOP on a tax-deductible basis, it will be possible to cover the shortfall with S corporation distributions.

Another strategy for dealing with the lower contribution limits available for S corporation ESOPs is simply to extend the term of the ESOP loan, to the point where the annual contribution required to service the debt falls within the 25% limit. This can be accomplished under a "back-to-back" loan structure, pursuant to which the plan sponsor borrows funds from an outside lender on normal commercial terms (with, for example, a seven-year amortization period), and the plan sponsor then loans the borrowed funds to the ESOP on extended payment terms (for example, a 15-year amortization period). No prepayment penalty should be provided for in the loan agreement between the plan sponsor and the ESOP, so that if the plan sponsor's covered payroll increases, the ESOP loan can be repaid more rapidly. The interest rate on the ESOP loan could be set at the minimum rate required to avoid triggering imputed interest, regardless of the interest payable to the outside lender, which will minimize the effect of the requirement that interest payments on an ESOP loan for an S corporation must be counted against the 25% limit.

Corporate-Level Tax

Another factor that an ESOP company should take into account in determining whether to make the S election is whether the election may

---

48. Code § 404(a)(9)(C).

49. Code § 404(a)(9)(B).

trigger unanticipated corporate-level taxation. Although as a general rule S corporations are not subject to tax, there are three exceptions. First, an S corporation that formerly was a C corporation is subject to tax on "built-in" gains recognized within 10 years of the effective date of the S election.[50] As discussed below, "built-in" gains are gains that are attributable to the period before the effective date of the S election.[51] If an ESOP company anticipates selling its assets or liquidating within 10 years from the date of the S election, the built-in gain tax may substantially diminish the benefits of the S election.

A second corporate-level tax to which an S corporation may be subjected is a LIFO "recapture" tax. When a C corporation which uses the LIFO inventory method makes the S election, it must include as income, over a four-year period, the excess of the value of its inventory determined on a FIFO basis over its value determined on a LIFO basis.[52] Finally, a corporation that makes the S election may be subject to tax on "excess net passive income."[53] ESOP companies that derive substantial amounts of their income from passive sources, such as rents, royalties, dividends, and interest, should evaluate the possible imposition of this tax before making the S election.

Compliance with Anti-Abuse Rules

An S corporation sponsoring an ESOP is required to comply with special anti-abuse rules discussed below. Failure to plan for and comply with these anti-abuse rules can result in the imposition of onerous taxes and penalties.

The 100% ESOP-Owned S Corporation

As discussed above, the tax savings and corporate cash-flow enhancements that can be obtained by an ESOP company that makes the S election are maximized when the ESOP owns all of the outstanding

---

50. Code § 1374.
51. Code § 1374(d).
52. Code § 1363(d).
53. Code § 1375.

stock of the corporation. For this reason, many ESOP companies have arranged for the buyout of all of their shareholders other than the ESOP, and a number of companies that have adopted ESOPs in recent years have arranged for the ESOP to obtain 100% ownership in one transaction. Complex financing arrangements are necessary to arrange for a 100% or near-100% ESOP buyout of a company, and once an S corporation becomes 100% ESOP-owned, it generally is necessary to develop equity incentive compensation arrangements for management other than traditional stock options and stock-based plans.

Financing the 100% ESOP Transaction

The majority of the funding for a 100% ESOP buyout of a company typically is comprised of a senior credit facility provided by one or more banks or other institutional lenders. The remainder of the financing typically is obtained from one or more of the following sources: institutional subordinated or "mezzanine" lenders; the selling shareholders; a private equity firm or other source of equity capital; or the employees themselves, via transfers of funds from other tax-qualified employee benefit plans. Where either mezzanine lending or seller financing is involved in a transaction, it typically is necessary for the borrower to pay a higher rate of interest on the subordinated loan than on the senior indebtedness, reflecting the greater risk being assumed by the subordinated lender; and it also often is necessary to enhance the rate of return for the subordinated lender with an equity "kicker." Typically, the equity kicker takes the form of options to purchase stock of the borrower. These types of options generally are referred to as warrants. Where the borrower is an S corporation, it is important to assure that warrants issued to subordinated lenders will not be treated as stock for federal income tax purposes. If the warrants are treated as stock, the company's S election will be terminated by reason of violation of the one-class-of-stock requirement because the warrants will have rights and preferences different from the rights and preferences associated with the common stock.

Fortunately, warrants issued by S corporations to lenders generally will not be treated as a second class of stock. The regulations provide that an option will not be treated as a second class of stock if it is issued to a person that is "actively and regularly engaged in the business of lending" and if the option is issued "in connection with a commercially reasonable loan to the corporation."[54] If seller financing is involved in an ESOP transaction, the following two conditions must be satisfied for any warrants issued to the sellers not to be treated as a second class of stock: (1) the warrants must not be "substantially certain to be exercised," and (2) the strike price for the warrants must not be substantially below the fair market value of the underlying stock on the date that the option is issued (or on the date that the warrants are transferred to a person who is not eligible to hold shares of an S corporation or the date upon which the warrants are "materially modified").[55]

In addition to the rules described above for determining whether a stock option or warrant issued by an S corporation will be treated as a second class of stock, there is a safe-harbor rule under which an option will not be treated as a second class of stock if, on the date that the option is issued, the strike price is at least 90% of the fair market value of the underlying stock.[56] The regulations provide that a good-faith determination of fair market value by the corporation will be respected "unless it can be shown that the value was substantially in error and the determination of the value was not performed with reasonable diligence to obtain a fair value."[57]

Even where some of the funding for a 100% ESOP buyout will be provided by a private equity firm or other equity source, it will be in the interest of all of the parties to structure the financing in the form of subordinated debt with warrants attached. As long as the warrants are properly structured so as to avoid being treated as a second class

---

54. Treas. Regs. § 1.1361-1(l)(4)(iii)(B)(1).

55. Treas. Regs. § 1.1361-1(l)(4)(iii)(A). If an option is issued in connection with a loan and the time period during which the option can be exercised is extended in connection with (and consistent with) a modification of the terms of the loan, then the extension of the time period during which the option may be exercised will not be considered to be a material modification.

56. Treas. Regs. § 1.1361-1(l)(4)(iii)(C).

57. Ibid. Failure of an option to satisfy these safe-harbor standards will not necessarily result in the option being treated as a second class of stock. Rather, the holder of the option simply will not be entitled to the presumption that the option is not stock provided by the safe-harbor rule.

of stock, the corporation then will retain its eligibility to make the S election and will not be required to make any earnings distributions to cover shareholder-level taxes.

Where some of the funding for an ESOP transaction will be provided by the employees by means of transfers from other tax-qualified plans, there will be no need to provide equity "enhancements," through the use of warrants or otherwise, because the employees will be able to hold equity interests through the ESOP. The funds that they invest in the transaction typically are transferred to the ESOP from a profit-sharing or Section 401(k) plan sponsored by the ESOP company. Although the employees' interests will be equity interests, these interests will not be a second class of stock. Rather, there will be allocated to their accounts stock of the same class as the other stock held by the ESOP. If an ESOP transaction is funded in part with transfers to the ESOP of account balances from other employee benefit plans, care must be taken to assure compliance with all applicable federal and state securities laws.[58]

Equity Incentives for Employees

Equity compensation arrangements for executives of 100% ESOP-owned S corporations generally must be designed in a way that does not involve actual grants of stock. If any of the executives become stockholders, they will be required to report a proportionate amount of the company's earnings on their personal income tax returns. In turn, this likely would require the corporation to distribute to the executives earnings in an amount sufficient to cover the taxes on their shares of the company's income, and the company then would be required to make proportionate distributions to the ESOP, as discussed above. The tax savings from the S election then would not result in enhanced cash flows to the company. Therefore, incentive compensation arrangements for executives of ESOP-owned S corporations generally take the form of stock options,[59] phantom stock, or stock appreciation rights.

---

58. For a discussion of the applicable federal and state securities law, see Maldonado, 362-3d T.M., *Securities Law Aspects of Employee Benefit Plans*.

59. Of course, once any of the options are exercised, the persons acquiring stock will become subject to tax on their share of the S corporation's income. This will raise the tax-distributions problem discussed above. Therefore, stock

Compensation planning for executives is further complicated in an ESOP-owned company because equity incentive arrangements, like warrants granted to subordinated lenders, must be carefully structured to avoid being treated as a second class of stock. Options granted by an S corporation to employees in connection with the performance of services will not be treated as a second class of stock if the following conditions are satisfied: (1) they are not excessive in comparison to the value of the services performed; (2) they are nontransferrable; and (3) they do not have a "readily ascertainable fair market value" at the time that they are issued.[60] Options issued by S corporations almost never will have a "readily ascertainable fair market value." Therefore, compliance with the one-class-of-stock rule in connection with the issuance by an S corporation of stock options generally can be assured by making the options nontransferrable.[61]

In addition to stock options, ESOP-owned S corporations also often use phantom stock or stock appreciation rights to compensate key executives. These types of so-called "synthetic equity" arrangements generally will not be treated as a second class of stock for federal income tax purposes. However, the use of these types of arrangements by ESOP-owned S corporations is limited by the anti-abuse rules described below.

Anti-Abuse Rules for S Corporation ESOPs

Perceived Abuses

Shortly after S corporations first became eligible to sponsor ESOPs in 1998, two abuses arose. The first abuse involved the adoption of ESOPs by S corporations that had only one or a few employees. For

---

option plans for employees of a 100% ESOP-owned corporation generally are structured in a way to provide for a cash-out of the options at their time of exercise. Similar arrangements typically are made for warrants issued to subordinated lenders who provide financing for 100% ESOP-owned companies.

60. Treas. Regs. § 1.1361-1(l)(4)(iii)(B)(2).

61. For a discussion of the tax treatment of stock options granted by S corporations, see David Ackerman, "Stock Options for S Corporations," *Journal of Employee Ownership Law and Finance* 13, no. 3 (summer 2001): 55.

example, a highly paid professional might seek to defer taxes indefinitely by incorporating his or her business and then transferring all of the stock of the corporation to an ESOP. The professional person would be the sole participant in the ESOP, and the sole purpose for setting up the ESOP would be to defer tax on the income generated from the professional's business activities. This use of an ESOP obviously does not serve the policy underlying ESOP legislation, which is to promote broad-based employee ownership and thereby enhance employee productivity.

A second abuse of the use of ESOPs by S corporations involved a so-called "tax holiday" for newly formed enterprises, where executives and outside investors held stock options and other forms of equity interests which, over time, would substantially dilute the ESOP's ownership. The equity interests for the executives and outside investors could be designed in such a way as to defer their recognition of income over a period of several years, during which time all of the corporate earnings would be reported by the ESOP and thereby escape taxation (the "tax holiday"). If the ESOP will be substantially diluted after the stock options are exercised and the other equity interests vest, the ESOP will have served only to avoid taxes and not to promote employee ownership.[62]

To eliminate the two abuses described above and any similar tax avoidance schemes, Congress enacted a set of special anti-abuse rules for S corporation ESOPs, which are set forth in Section 409(p) of the Code. Under Section 409(p), an ESOP that holds shares of an S corporation is prohibited from allocating employer securities to certain persons who are identified as "disqualified individuals" during any "nonallocation year."[63] The term "nonallocation year" means a year in which disqualified persons own at least 50% of the outstanding shares of the plan sponsor.[64]

---

62. For an example of how an abusive "tax holiday" transaction might have been structured, see Ginsburg, "The Taxpayer Relief Act of 1997: Worse Than You Think," *Tax Notes* 76 (Sept. 29, 1997): 1790.

63. Code § 409(p)(1).

64. Code § 409(p)(3).

Disqualified Persons

For purposes of Section 409(p), a person is a "disqualified person" if either (1) he or she is deemed to own 10% or more of the "deemed-owned shares" of the corporation, or (2) the aggregate number of shares deemed to be owned by the person, together with the shares deemed to be owned by members of his or her family, is at least 20% of the total deemed-owned shares of the corporation.[65] A participant in an S corporation ESOP is deemed to own shares that are allocated to his or her ESOP account and a portion of the shares which are held in the suspense account and that have not been allocated to participants' accounts.[66] A participant's share of unallocated stock is the amount of that stock that would be allocated to him or her if the unallocated stock were allocated to all participants in the plan in the same proportion as the most recent stock allocation under the plan.[67]

In addition, an individual who owns "synthetic equity" in an S corporation will be deemed to own the shares of stock on which the synthetic equity is based if this will result in the treatment of him or her as a disqualified person.[68] The term "synthetic equity" is defined to mean any stock option, warrant, restricted stock, deferred issuance stock right, or similar interest or right that gives the holder the right to acquire or receive stock of the S corporation in the future.[69] The term "synthetic equity" also includes stock appreciation rights, phantom

---

65. Code § 409(p)(4).

66. Code § 409(p)(4)(C)(i).

67. Code § 409(p)(4)(C)(ii).

68. Code § 409(p)(5). The regulations interpreting Section 409(p) of the Code make it clear that the determination whether someone is a disqualified person is made by way of a two-step analysis: first without regard to any synthetic equity attributable to that person and, second, by taking synthetic equity into account. Treas. Reg. § 1.409(p)-1(d)(1).

69. Code § 409(p)(6)(C). In Revenue Ruling 2004-4 (2004-6 I.R.B.), the IRS held that rights to acquire stock in entities related to the plan sponsor also could be treated as synthetic equity. The ruling set forth three different situations involving S corporation ESOPs in which subsidiary stock options were used to enable certain individuals to obtain tax benefits associated with S corporation status, while severely limiting the ESOP's ability to benefit from the company's profits.

stock units, and similar rights to future cash payments based on the value of stock or growth in the value of stock.[70]

In determining whether an individual is a "disqualified person," only shares held for the benefit of the individual through the ESOP or on which synthetic equity is based count as "deemed-owned shares." Shares held outright by an individual, outside of the ESOP, are *not* "deemed-owned shares."

> *Example 2.* Corporation X is an S corporation. It has 10,000 shares outstanding, 7,000 of which are held by an ESOP. Arthur is a participant in the ESOP, and 600 shares are allocated to his ESOP account. Arthur's nephew, Bob, also is a participant in the ESOP, and 450 shares are allocated to his ESOP account. In addition, Bob owns 2,000 shares of X outside the ESOP. There are 4,000 shares of X remaining in the ESOP loan suspense account. Last year, 5% of the total shares released from the suspense account were allocated to Arthur's company stock account, and 3% of the total shares released from the suspense account were allocated to Bob's company stock account. Arthur is deemed to own 800 shares—the 600 shares allocated to his company stock account, plus 200 of the suspense account shares (4,000 x 5%). Arthur is a disqualified person, because his 800 deemed-owned shares constitute more than 10% of the total of 7,000 deemed-owned shares. Bob, however, is not a disqualified person, because he is deemed to own only 570 shares—the 450 shares allocated to his company stock account, plus 120 of the suspense account shares (400 x 3%). Application of the family aggregation rules to Bob does not result in his becoming a disqualified person, because the total number of the deemed-owned shares held by Arthur (800) plus Bob (570) is less than 20% of the 7,000 total deemed-owned shares. The 200 shares that Bob owns outside the ESOP are not counted in calculating the number of shares that he is deemed to own.[71]

> *Example 3.* Corporation Y is an S corporation. It has 10,000 shares outstanding, all of which are held by an ESOP and are allocated to the accounts of the participants in the plan. Cindy and Debbie are participants in the plan. Cindy has 625 shares allocated to her ESOP account, and Debbie has 1,000 shares allocated to her account. Cindy has an option to purchase 1,000 shares of Y's stock. In determining whether Cindy is a disqualified person, she is deemed to own both the 625 shares allocated to her ESOP account plus the 1,000

---

70. Ibid. See also Treas. Reg. § 1.409(p)-1(f)(2)(ii).

71. Examples 2 through 7 are based on examples that were developed by Luis Granados, whose assistance in the preparation of this chapter is gratefully acknowledged.

shares covered by her option. In determining the percentage of her ownership of the deemed-owned shares, the denominator of her fractional interest is 11,000 (the 10,000 outstanding shares held by the ESOP, plus the 1,000 shares covered by Cindy's option). Cindy's ownership is 14.8% (1,625 ÷ 11,000), which makes Cindy a disqualified person. Debbie also is a disqualified person because she is deemed to own 1,000 of 10,000 deemed-owned shares, which is 10% of the total deemed-owned shares. The 1,000 shares covered by Cindy's option are not taken into account in determining the percentage of deemed owned shares held by Debbie.[72] For purposes of determining whether there is a nonallocation year, both Cindy's and Debbie's shares will be included in the computation.

Nonallocation Year

If an S corporation sponsors an ESOP and any of the participants in the ESOP or any holders of synthetic equity are "disqualified persons," then there will be a nonallocation year, and the penalty taxes set forth in Section 409(p) of the Code will be triggered, if these disqualified persons own at least 50% of the outstanding shares of the corporation.[73] In determining whether the disqualified persons own 50% or more of the outstanding shares, there must be counted not only the shares actually owned by the disqualified persons, but also their "deemed-owned" shares plus shares that they are considered to own for federal income tax purposes under attribution-of-ownership rules.[74] Under these rules, an individual is considered as owning stock that is held by his or her spouse and by his or her children, grandchildren, and parents.[75] Moreover, for purposes of Section 409(p), an individual also will be considered to own shares held by any of his or her brothers or sisters, or brothers-in-law or sisters-in-law, or by any children or grandchildren of any brother or sister or brother-in-law or sister-in-law.[76] Individuals also are considered to own shares that are held in partnerships, estates, trusts, and corporations that they control.[77]

---

72. Treas. Reg. § 1.409(p)-1(d)(1)(ii).

73. Code § 409(p)(3)(A).

74. Code § 409(p)(3)(B).

75. Code § 318(a).

76. Code §§ 409(p)(3)(B)(i)(I), 409(p)(4)(D).

77. Code § 318(a).

Putting all these rules together, in order to determine whether an S corporation is subject to Section 409(p), the holdings of equity interests in the company should be analyzed as follows:

1. *Step One:* determine whether any of the participants in the ESOP or any of the holders of synthetic equity are disqualified persons:

    a. determine whether any participants in the ESOP or any of the holders of synthetic equity will be deemed to own at least 10% of the total number of deemed-owned shares; and

    b. determine whether any of the participants in the ESOP or any of the holders of synthetic equity are disqualified persons by reason of aggregate deemed ownership by the participant or synthetic equity holder and by members of his or her family of at least 20% of the total number of deemed-owned shares.

2. *Step Two:* determine the aggregate amount of shares owned or deemed to be owned by all of the disqualified persons, taking into account both the attribution-of-ownership rules and the synthetic-equity rules.

The second step of the analysis must be applied twice—once without taking synthetic equity into account and once with synthetic equity taken into account. First, if the number of the outstanding shares of the company owned or deemed to be owned by the disqualified persons (excluding all synthetic equity) is at least 50% of the corporation's total outstanding shares at any time during any plan year, then that year is a nonallocation year. Second, if the disqualified persons own or are deemed to own (including their synthetic equity share equivalents) at least 50% of the total outstanding shares plus the total synthetic equity share equivalents held by disqualified persons (but excluding synthetic equity share equivalents held by other persons), then the year will be a nonallocation year.[78]

> *Example 4.* Corporation Z is an S corporation, and it has 1,000 shares outstanding, all of which are held by an ESOP. Ellen has an option to acquire 1,050 shares, and Frank has an option to acquire 100 shares. Neither Ellen

---

78. Treas. Reg. § 1.409(p)-1(c)(1)(ii)(B).

nor Frank are participants in the ESOP, and they are not related to each other or to any of the ESOP participants. No ESOP participant has a large enough allocation to be a disqualified person. Ellen is a disqualified person because she owns more than 10% of the deemed-owned shares through her synthetic equity.[79] Frank is not a disqualified person because he owns less than 10% of the deemed-owned shares. The company passes the first test for avoiding a nonallocation year because the only disqualified person (Ellen) owns less than 50% of the outstanding shares—she owns none of them. The company fails the second test, however, because Ellen owns more than 50% of the sum of the total of outstanding shares plus shares of synthetic equity held by disqualified persons—1,050 out of a total of 2,050 shares. If the shares covered by Frank's option could be counted, then there would not be a nonallocation year, because Ellen would own 1,050 out of 2,150 total shares. However, the regulations clearly provide that synthetic equity held by persons who are not disqualified persons is excluded from the computation.[80]

Synthetic Equity

Buy-Sell Agreements
The treatment of synthetic equity has been a source of confusion under Section 409(p). Problems of interpretation are presented by the broad definition of the term "synthetic equity." The statute provides that this term includes *any* option or right to acquire shares, not merely the right to acquire newly issued shares.[81] Therefore, the law might be interpreted to mean that a person who has the right to purchase outstanding shares from a shareholder, such as on the death of the shareholder, will be deemed to own the number of shares he or she has the option to acquire. This could present a trap for the unwary, since there is no abuse presented by an option to acquire already-outstanding shares (because this will not dilute the ESOP).

The regulations interpreting Section 409(p) provide helpful guidance by providing that a right to acquire stock of an S corporation that is held by persons other than the ESOP, the S corporation, or a related

---

79. The shares covered by Frank's option cannot be counted in determining whether Ellen is a disqualified person. Only Ellen's synthetic equity can be counted for this purpose. Treas. Reg. § 1.409(p)-1(d)(1)(ii).

80. Treas. Reg. § 1.409(p)-1(c)(1).

81. Code § 409(p)(6)(C).

entity do not constitute synthetic equity.[82] Therefore, a disqualified person should not be treated as owning shares that he or she may be entitled to purchase pursuant to the terms of a conventional buy-sell agreement or pursuant to any other similar agreement restricting the transferability of stock. However, the regulations also provide that although rights to acquire already-outstanding shares will not be treated as synthetic equity, a disqualified person may be treated as owning other shares that he or she has the right to purchase.[83] This provision of the regulations presumably covers options and other rights with respect to treasury shares or rights to be issued by the corporation in the future. Fortunately, the regulations go on to provide that a disqualified person will not be treated as owning shares that he or she may be entitled to purchase pursuant to the terms of a conventional buy-sell agreement, or pursuant to any other similar agreement restricting the transferability of stock, unless either (1) a principal purpose of the agreement is to circumvent the one-class-of-stock requirement for S corporations, or (2) the agreement establishes a purchase price that, at the time that the agreement is entered into, is significantly in excess of or below the fair market value of the stock.[84]

Stock Options

In the case of stock options and other forms of synthetic equity the value of which is determined by reference to and payable in shares of stock, the person who is entitled to the synthetic equity is treated as owning the number of shares of stock to be delivered pursuant to the terms of the synthetic equity agreement.[85] In the case of synthetic equity for which payment is made in cash or other property (besides stock of the S corporation), the number of shares of synthetic equity treated as owned by the holder of the synthetic equity is equal to that number of shares of stock having a value equal to the cash or other property to be delivered.[86] In the case of stock appreciation rights, the number

---

82. Treas. Reg. § 1.409(p)-1 (f)(2)(i).
83. Treas. Reg. § 1.409(p)-1(c)(4)(i).
84. Treas. Reg. § 1.409(p)-1(c)(4)(ii).
85. Treas. Reg. § 1.409(p)-1(f)(4)(iii).
86. Ibid.

of synthetic equity shares is equal to the appreciation in the value of the stock by reference to which the rights are valued.[87]

> *Example 5*. George is granted stock appreciation rights with respect to 1,000 shares of S corporation stock. At the time of the grant of the rights, the value of the stock is $10 per share. At a specified future date, George will be entitled to a benefit equal to the difference between the value of 1,000 shares of stock at that time and their value at the date of the grant of the rights. If the value of the stock is $12.50 per share on the determination date, George would be treated as holding 200 shares of synthetic equity (the value of the stock appreciation rights of $2.50 per share, or $2,500 in total, divided by the value of $12.50 per share on the determination date).

Special Rule Relating to Voting Rights

The regulations add a special rule relating to voting rights. If a synthetic equity right includes a right to purchase or receive shares of S corporation stock that have greater voting rights on a per-share basis than the shares held by the ESOP, then the number of deemed-owned shares attributable to the synthetic equity will be at least equal to the number of shares that would have the same voting rights if those shares had the same per-share voting rights as the voting rights of the shares held by the ESOP.[88]

> *Example 6*. If shares of S corporation stock held by an ESOP are entitled to one vote per share, then an individual who holds an option to purchase one share with 100 votes is treated as owning 100 shares of synthetic equity.

Proportionality Rule

The regulations also provide that the number of shares deemed to be owned by a holder of synthetic equity is to be determined on a proportionate basis where the ESOP does not own all of the stock of the S corporation.[89] The application of this rule can be illustrated by the following example:

---

87. Ibid.

88. Treas. Reg. § 1.409(p)-1(f)(4)(v).

89. Treas. Reg. § 1.409(p)-1(f)(4)(iv).

Example 7. Assume that an S corporation has 10,000 shares outstanding and that Helen owns 2,500 shares and the ESOP owns the remaining 7,500 shares. Assume that Ira would be treated as owning 200 synthetic equity shares but for the special rule provided for situations where the ESOP does not own all of the stock of the S corporation. The number of synthetic equity shares treated as owned by Ira is decreased from 200 to 150, because the ESOP owns only 75% of the outstanding stock of the corporation.

Deferred Compensation

While the language of Section 409(p) limits the term "synthetic equity" to rights to acquire stock of the plan sponsor and rights to future cash payments based on the value of the stock of the plan sponsor, the regulations go further and provide that a deferred compensation arrangement will be treated as synthetic equity, even if it is neither payable in stock of the plan sponsor nor calculated by reference to the value of the stock of the plan sponsor.[90] The value of a deferred compensation arrangement is determined by converting the dollar value of the deferred compensation into an equivalent number of shares of stock in the plan sponsor, based on the present value of the interest or right to the deferred compensation and the fair market value of the plan sponsor's shares on the determination date.[91] A special rule limits the need for continual revaluation of deferred compensation synthetic equity by permitting triennial determination dates.[92]

This expansion of the synthetic equity concept is a response by the Treasury Department to abuses of the S corporation ESOP rules that have been promoted by aggressive tax and insurance advisors. One common technique that has been promoted involves the use of management companies. In a typical scheme, the owners of a profitable company ("C") create a new management company ("M"), and the owner-employees of C become employees of M. M then enters into an agreement to provide management services to C, in consideration for a fee based on C's performance. M makes the S election for federal income tax purposes and adopts an ESOP, to which all of the stock of M is contributed or sold for a nominal amount. The ESOP covers all

---

90. Treas. Reg. § 1.409(p)-1(f)(2)(iv).

91. Treas. Reg. § 1.409(p)-1(f)(4)(iii).

92. Treas. Reg. § 1.409(p)-1(f)(4)(ii)(C).

of the employees of both M and C. M then adopts a generous deferred compensation program for its employees, who are the principal shareholders of C. Under this scheme, C will deduct the management fees that it pays to M, as business expenses, and M then will use the fees to fund its deferred compensation program.

The management fees received by M constitute taxable income; but because M is an S corporation wholly owned by an ESOP, neither M nor its sole shareholder (the ESOP) is liable for any taxes. In essence, the scheme is designed to enable the C/M combined entity to obtain a current deduction for funding the owners' deferred compensation program, something that ordinarily is not allowed under U.S. federal income tax laws. The resulting tax savings theoretically could be enormous. While the employees will participate in the ESOP, their benefits will be minimal because most of the profits from business operations will be diverted into the deferred compensation fund for the owners. The regulations eliminate this obvious abuse of the S corporation ESOP rules because the deferred compensation will be treated as synthetic equity. As a result, the executives covered by the deferred compensation program will be treated as disqualified persons, and each taxable year of the S corporation will be a nonallocation year.[93]

Prohibited Allocations

If there is a nonallocation year and Section 409(p) applies, then no shares of the company's stock may be allocated for that year to the accounts of any disqualified persons (and no other assets may be allocated to their accounts in lieu of company stock, either under the ESOP or under any other tax-qualified plan that the company sponsors).[94] The regulations provide that the Section 409(p) prohibition has two elements: (1) a prohibition on "accruals," and (2) a prohibition on "allocations." In explaining how these two prohibitions work, the regulations create two new terms: "impermissible accrual" and "imper-

---

93. For a more thorough discussion of this tax-avoidance technique and how it can be attacked by the IRS, see David Ackerman, "New Anti-Abuse Rules for S Corporation ESOPs," *ESOP Report*, July 2001.

94. Code § 409(p)(1).

missible allocation."[95] If there is either an impermissible accrual or an impermissible allocation, then there is a prohibited allocation within the meaning of Section 409(p).[96]

An impermissible accrual occurs if any S corporation stock owned by the ESOP, or any assets attributable to that stock, are held for the benefit of a disqualified person during a nonallocation year.[97] For example, any S corporation stock held in a disqualified person's account would be counted as an impermissible accrual, even if the stock already had been allocated in a prior year.[98] In addition, any distributions made on, and any proceeds from the sale of, S corporation stock would constitute impermissible accruals.[99] An impermissible allocation is any allocation for a disqualified person under any tax-qualified plan of the employer that occurs during a nonallocation year to the extent that an allocation is made that, but for a provision in the ESOP to comply with Section 409(p), would have been added to the account of the disqualified person under the ESOP and invested in S corporation securities owned by the ESOP.[100]

Penalties for Violation of the Nonallocation Rules

If prohibited allocations are made to disqualified persons, then the company will be subject to an excise tax equal to 50% of the amount of the prohibited allocations,[101] and the shares allocated to the accounts of the disqualified persons will be treated as having been distributed to the disqualified persons and they will be subject to tax on the value of those shares.[102] The regulations seem to imply that these penalties are imposed for each nonallocation year, regardless of whether anything

---

95. Treas. Reg. § 1.409(p)-1(b)(2).

96. Treas. Reg. § 1.409(p)-1(b)(2)(i).

97. Treas. Reg. § 1.409(p)-1(b)(2)(ii).

98. Ibid.

99. Ibid.

100. Treas. Reg. § 1.409(p)-1(b)(2)(iii).

101. Code § 4979A(a).

102. Code § 409(p)(2)(A).

is added to the disqualified person's account for that year,[103] although this result seems contrary to the general structure of the statute, which differentiates between the penalties for the initial nonallocation year and the penalties for subsequent nonallocation years.[104] The statute does not specify how shares that are deemed to have been distributed are to be treated in future years. If they are treated as continuing to be held by the persons to whom they were deemed to have been distributed, then those persons will be personally liable for tax on their proportionate share of the S corporation's income.

In addition to the penalties described above, it is possible that if prohibited allocations are made by an S corporation ESOP, the ESOP then may be disqualified. The law requires that the plan document must prohibit allocations to disqualified persons during nonallocation years, so any prohibited allocation would violate the plan document.[105]

The IRS takes the position that violation of a plan document results in disqualification of the plan.[106] If an S corporation ESOP is disqualified, then the ESOP no longer would be a permitted holder of S corporation stock,[107] and the corporation's S election would be automatically terminated. There is a footnote in the legislative history of Section 409(p) which states that this result is not the Congressional intent,[108] but it is not known what position the IRS will take on this matter.

Additional penalties will be imposed if any synthetic equity is owned by a disqualified person in any nonallocation year. Then the company will be subject to an excise tax equal to 50% of the value of the shares on which the synthetic equity is based.[109] It is important to note that the tax is imposed on the value of the shares to which

---

103. Treas. Reg. § 1.409(p)-1(b)(2)(i)-(iii).

104. See Code § 4979A(e)(2)(C), which imposes an excise tax during the first nonallocation year of an S corporation ESOP by taking into account the total value of all of the deemed-owned shares of all disqualified persons.

105. Code § 409(p)(1).

106. See, e.g., Rev. Proc. 2001-17, § 5.01(2), defining the term "Qualification Failure" as "any failure that adversely affects the qualification of a plan," including a failure to follow plan provisions.

107. Code § 1361(c)(6)(A).

108. House Conference Report 107-84, May 26, 2001, § VI.4(g), n. 122.

109. Code § 4974A(a)(4).

the synthetic equity relates, and not the value of the synthetic equity itself.[110] Therefore, a substantial tax may be assessed even where the synthetic equity itself is of little or no value, as for example where the strike price with respect to an option is equal to or greater than the fair market value of the stock covered by the option. The tax on synthetic equity appears to be especially onerous because the tax appears to be imposed on the same synthetic equity for every nonallocation year. For the first nonallocation year of an S corporation ESOP, a 50% excise tax will be applied against the total value of all of the deemed-owned shares of all of the disqualified persons, regardless of the amount actually allocated to their accounts during that year[111]

Avoidance or Evasion of Section 409(p)

Section 409(p) of the Code authorizes the Treasury Department to issue regulations providing that a nonallocation year occurs in any case in which "the principal purpose of the ownership structure of an S corporation constitutes an avoidance or evasion of Section 409(p)."[112] Pursuant to this authority, the Treasury Department has set forth in the regulations the following standard for determining whether the principal purpose of the ownership structure of an S corporation involving synthetic equity constitutes an avoidance or evasion of Section 409(p): "whether, to the extent of the ESOP's stock ownership, the ESOP receives the economic benefits of ownership in the S corporation that occur during the period that stock of the S corporation is owned by the ESOP."[113] Among the factors identified in the regulations to be considered in determining whether the ESOP receives these economic benefits are shareholder voting rights, the right to receive distributions made to shareholders, and the right to benefit from the profits earned by the S corporation. In evaluating these factors, the regulations provide that there shall be taken into account the extent to which actual distributions of profits are made from the S corporation to the ESOP and the extent to which

---

110. Code § 4979A(e)(2)(B).

111. Code § 4979A(e)(2)(C).

112. Code § 409(p)(7)(B).

113. Treas. Reg. § 1.409(p)-(1)(g)(2).

the ESOP's ownership interest in undistributed profits and future profits is subject to dilution as a result of synthetic equity.[114]

The regulations go on to identify certain specific transactions that will be deemed to constitute an avoidance or evasion of Section 409(p). These transactions are the ones described in Revenue Ruling 2004-4, which involve fact patterns relating to the use of S corporation subsidiaries and other pass-through entities to enable certain individuals to benefit from the plan sponsor's S corporation status while limiting the ESOPs ability to benefit from the sponsor's profits.[115]

Prevention of Prohibited Allocations

There are several steps that might be taken by an S corporation that sponsors an ESOP to prevent an individual from becoming a disqualified person and to thereby avoid a nonallocation year. These measures include the following:

- reducing the amount of synthetic equity (for example, by canceling or distributing some or all of it);

- selling the S corporation stock held in the participant's ESOP account, so that the account is not invested in S corporation stock;

- distributing the S corporation stock held in the participant's account from the ESOP to the participant;

- transferring the S corporation stock held for the participant under the ESOP into a separate portion of the plan that is not an ESOP or to another qualified plan sponsored by the employer; or

- reshuffling account balances in a way designed to prevent participants from becoming disqualified persons.

A sale or distribution of S corporation stock allocated to a participant's account, or a transfer of S corporation stock allocated to a participant's account to another plan, might be deemed to violate the general nondiscrimination requirements applicable to all tax-quali-

---

114. Ibid.
115. Treas. Reg. § 1.409(p)-(1)(h).

fied employee benefit plans. This is because the sale, distribution, or transfer would not be made generally available to all participants in the plan. The regulations provide relief from the nondiscrimination requirements for a transfer of S corporation stock from an ESOP to another tax-qualified plan made for the purpose of assuring compliance with Section 409(p).[116] However, it should be noted that the other plan would be subject to unrelated business income tax on its share of the plan sponsor's income. ESOPs are the only type of employee benefit plans that are exempt from this tax.

Another possible approach would be to incorporate "fail-safe" language into an ESOP. This approach would require a change in the ESOP trust asset mix among participant accounts so as to not only prohibit allocations to disqualified persons during nonallocation years, but also to assure that the disqualified persons will not hold more than 50% of the total outstanding and deemed-owned shares of the corporation. This would work only with a careful review both of allocations of company stock within the ESOP and of ownership of company stock and of synthetic equity outside the ESOP. Just as a transfer of S corporation stock allocated from one participant's account to another plan might be deemed to violate the general non-discrimination requirements applicable to all tax-qualified employee benefit plans, if only one or a few persons' accounts are affected by the reshuffling of account balances, the nondiscrimination requirements may be violated. The fact that the regulations specifically authorize a plan-to-plan transfer, but not a reshuffling of the plan assets, may give rise to an inference that the reshuffling technique is not exempt from the nondiscrimination requirements.

The S Corporation Election

Taxation of S Corporations and Their Shareholders

The primary effect of the S election is that all items of an S corporation's income and loss are passed through to the corporation's shareholders.[117] There is allocated to each shareholder his or her proportionate

---

116. Treas. Reg. § 1.409(p)-1(b)(2)(v)(B).

117. Code § 1366.

share of each item of corporate income, deduction, loss, and credit.[118] The S corporation itself generally will not be subject to federal income tax.[119] A shareholder's basis in his or her stock of an S corporation is increased by his or her share of the corporate income and is decreased by distributions received by the shareholder from the corporation and by his or her share of the corporation's items of loss and deduction.[120] A shareholder's basis in stock of an S corporation may not be reduced below zero.[121] Distributions from S corporations to their shareholders generally are tax-free to the extent of the shareholders' bases in their stock.[122] A shareholder will be subject to tax on any distribution to the extent that it exceeds his or her stock basis.[123]

Eligibility to Make S Election

Speaking generally, the following requirements must be met by a corporation for it to be eligible to make the S election:[124]

- The corporation may not have more than 100 shareholders.
- All shareholders must be U.S. citizens or U.S. residents, and they must be natural persons, estates, or certain types of trusts (including employee benefit trusts).
- The corporation may have only one class of stock outstanding (but different voting rights are permitted for different shares of stock).[125]

In addition, the following types of corporations are ineligible to make the S election: financial institutions that use the reserve method of accounting for bad debts; insurance companies; certain so-called

---

118. Code § 1366(a).

119. Code § 1363(a).

120. Code § 1367(a).

121. Code § 1367(a)(2).

122. Code § 1368(c).

123. Code § 1368(b)(2).

124. Code § 1361(b).

125. Code § 1361(c)(4).

"possession corporations" (corporations that derive most of their income from sources within a possession of the United States); and domestic international sales corporations (DISCs).[126]

Advantages of S Corporation Election

Avoidance of Double Tax

An important tax advantage of the S election is that only one tax is imposed on the earnings of an S corporation. C corporations are subject to a "double tax"—once at the corporate level[127] and again at the shareholder level when the after-tax corporate earnings are distributed to the shareholders.[128] Many closely held C corporations have been able to avoid the double tax by distributing earnings to their shareholders in the form of tax-deductible compensation.[129] However, this is not a complete answer to the double-tax problem for C corporations whose earnings exceed the amount that can be deemed to be "reasonable" compensation or for C corporations that have shareholders who are not actively involved in the conduct of their business operations. No deductions will be allowed to a corporation for salaries or bonuses paid to shareholder-employees that are in excess of a reasonable amount, with the result that the excessive "compensation" will be treated as a nondeductible dividend for federal income tax purposes.[130]

Tax Savings on the Sale or Liquidation of a Business

Shareholders of a C corporation are subject to a double tax upon a sale of their corporation's assets or a liquidation of their corporation. First, the corporation is subject to tax on the difference between the sale or

---

126. Code § 1361(b)(2).

127. Code § 11.

128. Code § 301.

129. See James P. Holden and A.L. Suwalsky, Jr., 202-3d T.M. *Reasonable Compensation,* and David Ackerman and Thomas J. Kinasz, "Tax Considerations in Organizing Closely Held Corporations," chapter 2 of *Closely Held Corporations* (Illinois Institute for Continuing Legal Education, 1990), at 2–12.

130. Ibid.

liquidation proceeds and its basis in its assets,[131] and then the shareholders are subject to an additional tax on the distribution of the after-tax proceeds.[132] The effect may be illustrated by the following example:

> *Example 8.* Assume that a liquidating corporation sells its assets in 2008 at a gain of $1 million and that the shareholders' aggregate bases for their stock equals the corporation's basis for its assets. A 35% corporate tax will be imposed upon the gain, leaving the corporation with after-tax profits of $650,000. Upon the distribution of the proceeds to the shareholders, an additional tax in the amount of $97,500 will be imposed (15% of $650,000), leaving the shareholders with after-tax proceeds of $552,500.

If the corporation in the above example were an S corporation, only one tax would be imposed. The tax would be imposed upon the shareholders at a maximum rate of 15%, with the result that the total tax would be $150,000, as compared to $447,500, and the after-tax profit available to the shareholders would be $850,000, as compared to $552,500. Table 2-1 summarizes the comparison in tax results.

If the transaction took the form of a liquidation, gain would be recognized by the corporation to the extent of the excess of the fair market value of its assets over the corporation's basis in its assets,[133] and the results would be the same. A double tax would be imposed on the C corporation and its shareholders, but only one level of tax would be imposed on the S corporation and its shareholders because the corporate gain would pass through to the shareholders, and their tax bases would be increased by the amount of the gain recognized.[134]

If the transaction took the form of a sale of stock, the corporate-level tax could be avoided even if the corporation had not made an S election, provided that the purchaser did not make an election under Section 338 of the Code to treat the transaction as a purchase of assets for federal income tax purposes. However, unless this election is made, the acquired corporation will not be entitled to step up the basis of its assets to the price paid for the stock. Then the amount of depreciation and amortization deductions to which the acquired corporation will

---

131. Code § 1001.

132. Code § 301.

133. Code § 336(a).

134. See footnotes 117–23 and accompanying text.

Table 2-1. Tax on Sale of Appreciated Property and Liquidation ($1,000,000 Taxable Gain)

C Corporation	
Corporate Gain	$1,000,000
Corporate Tax	(350,000)
After-Tax Corporate Profit	650,000
Tax on Distribution Less Basis (15% × $650,000)	(97,500)
After-Tax Profit	$ 552,500
Effective Tax Rate ([$1,000,000 − $552,500] ÷ $1,000,000)	44.75%
S Corporation	
Corporate Gain	$1,000,000
Corporate Tax	(0)
After-Tax Corporate Profit	1,000,000
Tax on Distribution Less Basis (15% × $1,000,000)	(150,000)
After-Tax Profit	$ 850,000
Effective Tax Rate ([$1,000,000 − $850,000] ÷ $1,000,000)	15.0%

be entitled in the future normally will be less than would be the case after a transaction structured as a purchase of assets.

On the other hand, if the purchaser makes the Section 338 election, the acquired corporation will be treated for tax purposes as if it had sold its assets and, as the new shareholder of the acquired corporation, the purchaser will bear the burden of the tax imposed on the constructive gain recognized by the acquired corporation. In order to both avoid this tax and obtain the benefit of a step-up in the basis of the acquired corporation's assets, a purchaser of a business normally will prefer to structure an acquisition as a purchase of assets and normally will pay a higher price for assets than for stock. Therefore, substantial benefits can be obtained by the owners of a corporation that will be sold by making an S election, even where it may be possible to arrange for a sale of their business in the form of a sale of stock.

To limit the benefits that can be obtained by converting a C corporation to an S corporation, Congress has enacted a corporate-level tax on S corporations that formerly were C corporations. This tax is imposed on any gain that arose before the effective date of the S election ("built-in" gain) and that is recognized by the S corporation within 10 years after the conversion by reason of a sale or distribution of its assets.[135] The built-in gain tax is assessed at a rate equal to the highest rate of corporate tax.[136] This tax applies in each year to the lesser of the S corporation's built-in gain or its taxable income.[137] Any recognized built-in gain not taxed by reason of the taxable-income limitation is carried forward to later tax years in which the S corporation has additional taxable income.[138]

To return to the above example, if the value of the assets of the corporation on the effective date of its S election had exceeded the corporation's basis in its assets by $500,000, it then would be subject to a corporate-level tax on $500,000 of the gain realized upon the sale of its assets. Because the built-in gain tax applies only to S corporations that previously were C corporations, the tax can be completely avoided if an S election is made at the time that a corporation is organized and is maintained in effect continually thereafter.

Pass-Through of Losses

Just as the earnings of an S corporation are "passed through" and taxed to its shareholders, so generally are its losses.[139] The shareholders may apply these losses to reduce their income from other sources, up to an amount equal to their tax bases in their stock.[140] Therefore, S elections often are made by owners of start-up ventures who desire the limited liability and other features of incorporation and who anticipate that losses will be incurred at the outset of their operations.[141] Losses of a C corporation may be used only to offset prior or future corporate income.[142]

---

135. Code § 1374. Congress has considered, but not yet passed, legislation that would impose the tax at the time that the S election is made. Budget of the U.S. Govt., FY 1998, Legislative Proposals (1997).

136. Code § 1374(b)(1).

137. Code § 1374(d)(2).

138. Code § 1374(d)(2)(B).

139. Code § 1366.

140. Code § 1366(d).

141. For a potentially abusive use of S corporation ESOPs to take advantage of the pass-through of losses of a start-up venture, see Ginsburg, "The Taxpayer Relief Act of 1997: Worse Than You Think," *Tax Notes* 76 (Sept. 29, 1997): 1790.

142. Code § 172(b).

Other Benefits

Other benefits of the S election include the following: avoidance of the corporate alternative minimum tax;[143] reduction of the risks of a challenge by the IRS to the amount of compensation paid to shareholders;[144] avoidance of the accumulated earnings tax;[145] and the availability of the cash method of accounting.[146]

---

143. Code § 1363(a). However, an S corporation shareholder may be subject to the alternative minimum tax as a result of the pass-through of items of tax preference of the S corporation. See Code § 1366(b).

144. Because an S corporation generally is not subject to the corporate tax, it generally makes no difference for tax purposes whether distributions to shareholders of S corporations are characterized as compensation or dividends. This does not mean, however, that there is no limit on the amount of compensation that may be paid to the corporation's officers. To the extent that the officers' compensation exceeds a reasonable amount, the shareholders of the corporation may be able to impose limits under applicable corporate laws. The board of directors of a corporation must act in the best interests of the shareholders in managing the affairs of the corporation, and directors who approve excessive officer compensation may be held liable for mismanagement. Where some or all of the shares of a corporation are held by an ESOP, the ESOP trustee should monitor the actions of the board of directors. Among other things, the ESOP trustee should evaluate the amount of compensation being paid to the officers. To the extent that the officers' compensation is excessive, corporate earnings to which the ESOP and the other shareholders otherwise would be entitled are being drained off to the officers. In that case, the ESOP trustee would have an obligation to take action to protect the interests of the ESOP. If necessary, the ESOP trustee might have a duty to bring a shareholders' derivative action against the directors. For a thorough discussion of the duties of an ESOP trustee in connection with the monitoring of management compensation, see David Ackerman, "Questions and Answers Regarding the Legal Responsibilities of ESOP Fiduciaries," *Journal of Employee Ownership Law & Finance* 13, no. 1 (winter 2001): 1, 31–32.

145. Code § 1363(a). Because S corporations generally are not subject to federal income tax and business earnings of an S corporation are taxed to the shareholders whether or not distributed, there is no reason to penalize accumulations of income in an S corporation.

146. Most regular corporations with annual gross receipts in excess of $5 million are prohibited from using the cash method of accounting. Code § 448. However, limitations on the use of the cash method of accounting do not apply to S corporations. Code § 448(a).

Disadvantages of S Corporation Election

Shareholder Limitations

An S corporation may have no more than 100 shareholders.[147] This may require a corporation to closely monitor and control the distribution of its stock. In addition, some investors may be frustrated by the limitations on the kinds of trusts that may hold stock of an S corporation.

One-Class-of-Stock Limitation

The one-class-of-stock limitation restricts planning options for the capital structure of an S corporation. For example, no preferred stock can be issued by an S corporation to outside investors. However, the issuance by an S corporation of most types of stock options, stock warrants, or convertible debentures generally will not constitute the creation of a second class of stock.[148] Many existing ESOP companies have capital structures that include convertible preferred stock or so-called "super" common stock, in addition to regular common stock. These kinds of shares often are issued where it is anticipated that dividends will be used to pay off an ESOP loan because the annual loan payments exceed the maximum amount that may be contributed to the plan on a tax-deductible basis. In this situation, it generally is desirable to limit the dividends to shares held by the ESOP. In this way, the dividend cost can be limited, and double taxation on dividends that otherwise would be payable to other shareholders can be avoided.[149] Where a C corporation has created a second class of stock for these reasons, it

---

147. Code § 1361(b)(1)(A).

148. Rev. Rul. 67-269, 1967-2 Cum. Bull. 298. See, e.g., Treas. Regs. §§ 1361-1(b)(4), 1361-1(l)(4)(iii). See discussion above at footnotes 54–61. See also David Ackerman, "Stock Options for S Corporations," *Journal of Employee Ownership Law and Finance* 13, no. 3 (summer 2001): 55.

149. For discussions of the use of "super" common and convertible preferred stocks in ESOPs, see Gregory K. Brown and Kim Schultz Abello, "ESOPs and Security Design: Common Stock, Super Common, or Convertible Preferred?" *Journal of Pension Planning & Compliance* 23 (1997): 99, and Jared Kaplan, "Is ESOP a Fable? Fabulous Uses and Benefits or Phenomenal Pitfalls?" *Taxes* 65 (1987): 792–93.

may not be feasible to make the S election, which would require the elimination of the special class of stock created for the ESOP.

Limitation on Other Benefits

Persons who own 2% or more of the outstanding shares of an S corporation may not exclude from their income the value of fringe benefits that are provided to them.[150] Examples of these types of benefits include group term life insurance, certain health and accident plans, death benefits, and meals and lodging reimbursement.

Fiscal Year

The taxable year of an S corporation must be the calendar year unless the corporation can establish, to the satisfaction of the IRS, a business purpose for using a different fiscal year.[151] Not surprisingly, the deferral of income to stockholders for a limited period of time will not be treated as a business purpose.[152] However, an S corporation may adopt a taxable year other than the calendar year if shareholders holding more than one-half of the shares of the corporation have the same tax year or are changing to the corporation's tax year.[153] This means that if an ESOP holds more than one-half of the outstanding shares of an S corporation, the S corporation may adopt the same taxable year as the ESOP, even if that year is not the calendar year. Where the principal shareholders of an S corporation are changing to a new tax year to be adopted by the corporation, the shareholders may not change their tax year without first obtaining approval from the IRS.[154] There is an

---

150. Code § 1372.

151. Code §§ 444, 1378. An example of a business purpose that will be accepted for adopting a taxable year other than the calendar year is a change to a tax year that coincides with the corporation's "natural business year." A taxable year will be deemed to be a natural business year if 25% or more of the corporation's gross receipts in each of the last three 12-month periods proposed to serve as the taxable year have been recognized in the last two months of those periods. Rev. Proc. 83-25 § 4.04, 1983-1 C.B. 689, 692.

152. Code § 1378(b).

153. Rev. Proc. 83-25 § 4.02, 1983-1 C.B. 689.

154. Ibid.

exception to the general rule under which an S corporation may elect to adopt a tax year ending not earlier than September 30.[155] In that case, however, payments in the nature of advance tax deposits are required, which takes away the advantage of the tax deferral.[156]

State Tax Considerations

Although most states recognize S corporation status for purposes of their tax laws, not all states follow the federal pattern. Some states tax S corporations and not their shareholders; some states tax both the S corporation and its shareholders; and some states do not tax either the corporation or the shareholders. If the S election is made by a corporation that is incorporated in a state that does not follow the federal rules regarding the tax treatment of S corporations or that has modified them, difficult state tax compliance programs can arise, especially if multi-state operations are involved.[157]

Conclusion

Enormous tax savings are possible for corporations that make the S election for federal income tax purposes and adopt an ESOP. These tax benefits are maximized where all of the outstanding shares of the corporation are held by the ESOP. In recent years there has been a significant increase in the number of companies that have become wholly owned by ESOPs and have made the S election. This trend can be expected to continue as understanding of the tax incentives created for ESOP-owned S corporations increases. As the number of ESOP-owned S corporations expands, Congress may reexamine the tax incentives that it has provided for this form of business ownership.[158] However, to date, the anti-abuse rules of Section 409(p) have

---

155. Code § 444(b).

156. Code §§ 444(c)(1), 7519.

157. For a thorough discussion of this issue, see Maule, *S Corporations: State Law and Taxation* (Deerfield, IL: Callaghan, 1992). Also see chapter 3 of this book, "A State-by-State Analysis of S Corporation Tax Treatment."

158. For example, at the time of the publication of this chapter, there was pending before Congress a proposal to greatly limit the use by ESOP-owned S

worked well. S corporations with few employees are unable to use ESOPs, and Section 409(p) prevents the creation of capital structures in ESOP-owned S corporations that can result in excessive dilution to the ESOP. As a result, the Congressional policy of promoting employee ownership is being fulfilled by the increase in the number of ESOP-owned S corporations.

corporations of synthetic equity arrangements for executives and investors (H.R. 3970).

CHAPTER THREE

A State-by-State Analysis of S Corporation Tax Treatment

Renee Lewis

Before 1998, ESOPs were not eligible to hold shares of an S corporation. The 1996 tax law amended the provisions of Subchapter S to allow ESOP companies to make the S election.[1] An S corporation generally is not subject to federal income tax.[2] Instead, the shareholders of the corporation are subject to tax on the corporation's earnings, whether they are distributed to them as dividends or retained in the corporation.[3] The primary effect of the S election is that all items of an S corporation's income and loss are passed through to the corporation's shareholders.[4] Each shareholder is allocated his or her proportionate share of each item of corporate income, deduction, loss, and credit.[5] An important tax advantage of the S election is that only one tax is imposed on the earnings of an S corporation. Regular or "C" corporations are subject to a "double tax"—once at the corporate level[6] and again at the shareholder level when the after-tax corporate earnings are distributed to shareholders.[7] An important tax advantage

---

1. Internal Revenue Code ("Code") § 1361(c)(6).
2. Code § 1363(a). See David Ackerman, et al., *S Corporation ESOPs*, 2nd ed. (NCEO, 2005).
3. Code § 1366(a).
4. Code § 1366.
5. Code § 1366(a).
6. Code § 11.
7. Code § 301.

of the S election where an ESOP is a shareholder is that an ESOP is a tax-exempt trust,[8] so any earnings attributable to the ESOP as a shareholder in the S corporation are tax-free.

Although most states recognize the federal S corporation election for purposes of their tax laws, many states impose additional requirements for state purposes. Some states require nonresident shareholders to consent to paying tax on their proportionate shares of the corporation's income; some states require a notice to be filed at the state level; some states allow corporations to opt out of federal S corporation treatment for state purposes; and some states require a separate state S corporation election to be made.

Once an S corporation election has been made, the tax treatment of the S corporation varies by state. Most states exempt an S corporation from income tax, but many states impose an income tax on the corporation (although often at a reduced rate). Even where a state exempts an S corporation from taxation, the state will frequently follow the federal provisions for taxes on built-in gains and passive investment income under Code Sections 1374 and 1375. Furthermore, most states do not exempt S corporations from franchise taxes based on net worth, and many states impose a franchise tax on S corporations that operate as financial institutions. Corporations may also need to consider the state tax treatment of qualified subchapter S subsidiaries ("QSubs"). A subsidiary is a QSub if the following requirements are met: (1) the subsidiary is a domestic corporation; (2) the subsidiary is not otherwise disqualified under Code Section 1361(b)(2); (3) 100% of the stock of the subsidiary is owned by an S corporation; and (4) the S corporation parent elects to treat the subsidiary as a QSub.[9] When an election to treat a subsidiary as a QSub is made, all assets, liabilities, and items of income, deduction, and credit of the QSub are treated as the assets, liabilities, and items of income of the parent S corporation.[10]

Corporations considering making an election to be treated as an S corporation should be aware of the state tax consequences before making the election. The question whether an ESOP company should

---

8.   Code § 501(a).

9.   Code § 1361(b)(3)(B).

10.   Code § 1361(b)(3)(A)(iii).

make an S election must be analyzed on a case-by-case basis, taking into consideration not only the federal tax benefits but also the tax consequences under state law.

This chapter analyzes the tax treatment of S corporations in each state. Table 3-1 sets forth (1) whether a state follows the federal S corporation election, (2) whether a state requires a separate state-level S election, (3) whether a state follows the federal treatment of QSubs, (4) whether a state holds an S corporation taxable or exempt for income tax purposes, and (5) whether a state imposes any other state taxes on an S corporation. The table is current as of December 31, 2007.

(Table 3-1 begins on next page)

Table 3-1. State-by-State Analysis

State	State Follows Federal S Corporation Election	Separate State Level S Election	State Follows Federal Treatment of Qualified Subchapter S Subsidiaries (QSubs)	Income Tax Treatment of S Corporations	Imposition of Other State Taxes on S Corporations
Alabama[1]	Yes	No	Yes	Exempt	Subject to AL business privilege tax
Alaska[2]	Yes	No	Yes	Exempt	
Arizona[3]	Yes	No	Yes	Exempt (to the extent that income is not subject to federal income tax)	
Arkansas[4]	Yes	Yes	Yes	Exempt	Subject to AR franchise tax
California[5]	Yes	No	Yes	Taxable (at a reduced rate)	Subject to CA franchise tax at a reduced rate (minimum franchise tax of $800)
Colorado[6]	Yes	No	Yes	Exempt	
Connecticut[7]	Yes	No	Yes	Exempt	Subject to the CT Business Entity Tax
Delaware[8]	Yes	No	Yes	Exempt	

(Notes to the table appear at the end of the article)

State	State Follows Federal S Corporation Election	Separate State Level S Election	State Follows Federal Treatment of Qualified Subchapter S Subsidiaries (QSubs)	Income Tax Treatment of S Corporations	Imposition of Other State Taxes on S Corporations
District of Columbia[9]	No (an S corporation under federal law is treated as a regular corporation for DC purposes)	No			
Florida[10]	Yes	No	No	Taxable	
			Yes	Exempt (to the extent income is not subject to federal income tax)	
Georgia[11]	Yes (election allowed only if all shareholders are subject to tax in GA on their portion of the corporate income and all nonresident shareholders pay GA income tax on their portion of the corporate income)	No (but must file a consent form for each nonresident shareholder where the shareholders agree to pay GA income tax on their proportionate share of the corporation's GA taxable income)	Yes (treatment applies for income tax purposes but not for net worth tax purposes)	Exempt	Nonresident shareholders are subject to withholding tax

State	State Follows Federal S Corporation Election	Separate State Level S Election	State Follows Federal Treatment of Qualified Subchapter S Subsidiaries (QSubs)	Income Tax Treatment of S Corporations	Imposition of Other State Taxes on S Corporations
Hawaii[12]	Yes	No	Yes	Exempt (to the extent income is not subject to federal income tax)	S corporation that is a financial corporation under HI law is subject to HI bank franchise tax
Idaho[13]	Yes	No	Yes	Exempt (except for tax on excess net passive income, capital gains, and built-in-gains))	
Illinois[14]	Yes	No	Yes	Exempt	Subject to IL replacement tax at a reduced rate
Indiana[15]	Yes	No	Yes	Exempt (except built-in gains and passive investment income subject to federal tax)	
Iowa[16]	Yes	No	Yes	Exempt (except built-in gains and passive investment income subject to federal tax)	S corporation that is a financial institution is subject to the IA financial institution franchise tax

State	State Follows Federal S Corporation Election	Separate State Level S Election	State Follows Federal Treatment of Qualified Subchapter S Subsidiaries (QSubs)	Income Tax Treatment of S Corporations	Imposition of Other State Taxes on S Corporations
Kansas[17]	Yes	No	Yes		S corporations that are banks and savings and loan associations are subject to KS bank privilege tax rather than KS income tax
Kentucky[18]	Yes	No	Yes	Exempt (except subject to tax on the same items of income and in the same manner as required for federal tax purposes)	Subject to limited liability entity tax

State	State Follows Federal S Corporation Election	Separate State Level S Election	State Follows Federal Treatment of Qualified Subchapter S Subsidiaries (QSubs)	Income Tax Treatment of S Corporations	Imposition of Other State Taxes on S Corporations
Louisiana[19]	No, but the corporation may be able to exclude income that is taxed to the shareholders based on the ratio of issued and outstanding shares owned by LA resident individuals to total issued and outstanding shares of the S corporation	N/A	Yes (if QSub qualifies for exclusion, S corporation that owns stock of QSub files a LA income tax return that includes all income of QSub)	Taxable (but may exclude a percentage of its LA net income for the taxable year)	
Maine[20]	Yes	No	Yes	Exempt (except subject to tax on built-in-gains and if the corporation has a resident shareholder or income derived from sources in ME)	S corporations that are financial institutions are subject to franchise tax

State	State Follows Federal S Corporation Election	Separate State Level S Election	State Follows Federal Treatment of Qualified Subchapter S Subsidiaries (QSubs)	Income Tax Treatment of S Corporations	Imposition of Other State Taxes on S Corporations
Maryland[21]	Yes	No	Yes	Exempt (to the extent income is not subject to federal income tax)	
	Yes (excluding corporate trusts, security corporations, and public utility corporations)			Exempt (to the extent income is not subject to federal income tax and provided entity has less than $6 million in gross receipts) Entity with $6 million or more in gross receipts is subject to corporate excise tax (measured by net income) at a reduced rate	Subject to the excise tax (not measured by net income) or, if applicable, the minimum excise tax
Massachusetts[22]		No	Yes		
Michigan[23]	No	No	Yes	Taxable (MI imposes the Single Business Tax rather than an income tax)	

State	State Follows Federal S Corporation Election	Separate State Level S Election	State Follows Federal Treatment of Qualified Subchapter S Subsidiaries (QSubs)	Income Tax Treatment of S Corporations	Imposition of Other State Taxes on S Corporations
Minnesota[24]	Yes	No		Exempt (except for tax on certain built-in-gains, capital gains, and passive investment income)	Subject to minimum fee
Mississippi[25]	Yes	Yes (within 60 days of filing Form 2553)	Yes		Subject to franchise tax
Missouri[26]	Yes	No	Yes	Exempt	Subject to franchise tax
Montana[27]	Yes	No	Yes	Exempt	
Nebraska[28]	Yes	No	Yes	Exempt	S corporation that is a financial institution may be subject to financial institution tax if certain requirements met

State	State Follows Federal S Corporation Election	Separate State Level S Election	State Follows Federal Treatment of Qualified Subchapter S Subsidiaries (QSubs)	Income Tax Treatment of S Corporations	Imposition of Other State Taxes on S Corporations
Nevada	Nevada does not impose an income tax on businesses.	N/A	N/A	N/A	N/A
New Hampshire[29]	No (S corporation under federal law treated same as regular corporation)	N/A	No (QSub under federal law treated as a regular S corporation for business profits tax purposes, must keep detailed records, and must file its own return unless part of a combined return)	Taxable	Subject to NH business enterprise tax
New Jersey[30]	Yes	Yes	Yes (QSub must meet certain additional requirements under NJ law)	Taxable (at a reduced rate)	
New Mexico[31]	Yes	No	Yes	Exempt	Subject to NM franchise tax

State	State Follows Federal S Corporation Election	Separate State Level S Election	State Follows Federal Treatment of Qualified Subchapter S Subsidiaries (QSubs)	Income Tax Treatment of S Corporations	Imposition of Other State Taxes on S Corporations
New York[32]	Yes	Yes	Yes	Taxable	
New York City [33]	No	Yes	No (QSub treated as separate corporation)	Taxable	
North Carolina[34]	Yes	No	Yes	Exempt	Subject to franchise tax
North Dakota[35]	Yes	No	Yes	Exempt (to the extent income not subject to federal income tax)	
Ohio[36]	Yes	No (although annual notice required)	Yes	Exempt from OH franchise tax (measured by net worth) Subject to OH commercial activity tax (measured by gross receipts)	

State	State Follows Federal S Corporation Election	Separate State Level S Election	State Follows Federal Treatment of Qualified Subchapter S Subsidiaries (QSubs)	Income Tax Treatment of S Corporations	Imposition of Other State Taxes on S Corporations
Oklahoma[37]	Yes	No	Yes	Exempt	Subject to franchise tax
Oregon[38]	Yes	No	Yes	Exempt (except subject to tax built-in-gain and excess net passive income)	Subject to a $10 minimum tax
Pennsylvania[39]	Yes	No (although to be a valid PA S corporation, must not make a valid election to opt out of treatment as a PA S corporation)	Yes	Exempt (except to the extent taxed on built-in-gains under federal law)	Subject to franchise tax
Rhode Island[40]	Yes	No	Yes	Exempt (to the extent income is not subject to federal income tax)	Subject to franchise tax

State	State Follows Federal S Corporation Election	Separate State Level S Election	State Follows Federal Treatment of Qualified Subchapter S Subsidiaries (QSubs)	Income Tax Treatment of S Corporations	Imposition of Other State Taxes on S Corporations
South Carolina[41]	Yes	No (but most notify Dept. of Rev. of intent to be S-corp)	Yes	Exempt (to the extent income is not subject to federal income tax)	Subject to the license fee
South Dakota	SD does not impose a tax measured by net income on businesses or individuals. Net income tax is imposed on financial institutions (even if S corporations).				
Tennessee[42]	No	N/A	No (QSub must file its own separate entity excise tax election)	Taxable	

State	State Follows Federal S Corporation Election	Separate State Level S Election	State Follows Federal Treatment of Qualified Subchapter S Subsidiaries (QSubs)	Income Tax Treatment of S Corporations	Imposition of Other State Taxes on S Corporations
Texas[43]	No	N/A	TX does not impose an income tax on businesses. S corporations are subject to a franchise tax in the same manner as regular corporations	Subject to franchise tax.	
Utah[44]	Yes	No	Yes	Exempt	
Vermont[45]	Yes	No	Yes	Exempt (except to the extent income is subject to federal income tax)	Subject to minimum tax of $250
Virginia[46]	Yes	No	Yes	Exempt	

State	State Follows Federal S Corporation Election	Separate State Level S Election	State Follows Federal Treatment of Qualified Subchapter S Subsidiaries (QSubs)	Income Tax Treatment of S Corporations	Imposition of Other State Taxes on S Corporations
Washington[47]	WA does not impose an income tax on businesses or individuals. S corporations are subject to WA Business and Occupation Tax	N/A			
West Virginia[48]	Yes	No	Yes	Exempt	Subject to franchise tax
Wisconsin[49]	Yes	No (but must not have elected out of tax-option corporation status)	Yes	Exempt (except to the extent it is taxed on net recognized built-in-gains for federal tax purposes)	Subject to WI recycling surcharge as a percentage of net income
Wyoming	WY does not impose an income tax on businesses or individuals.				

Notes to the Table

1. Ala. Code § 14A-22(a), § 40-18-160(a), § 40-18-160(b).

2. Alaska Stat. § 43.20.021(a), § 43.20.300(a), § 43.126(A).

3. Ariz. Rev. Stat. Ann. § 43-1126(A).

4. Ark. Code Ann. § 26-51-409(a), § 26-51-409(b); § 26-54-104.

5. Cal. Rev. & Tax. Cd. § 23153, § 23800, § 23800.5(a), § 23801(a), § 23802(c).

6. Colo. Rev. Stat. § 39-22-103(5.3), § 39-22.103(10.5), § 39-22-302, § 39-22-322(1).

7. Conn. Gen. Stat. § 12-213(a)(22), § 12-214(a)(2)(J), § 12-217(c)(2), § 12-284b(b)(6).

8. Del. Income Tax Reg. § 1.1900.2(b), (c) & (d); Del. Code Ann. tit 30, § 1601(a)(2), § 1621(a), § 1902(b)(9).

9. D.C. Code Ann. § 47-1801.04(16), § 47-1807.02.

10. Fla. Stat. Ann. § 220.02(9); Fla. Admin. Code Ann. § 12C-1.022(1)(b)(1).

11. Ga. Code Ann. § 47-7-27(d)(2), § 48-7-21(b)(7)(B); Ga. Comp. R. & Regs. § 560-7-3-.06(6)(a).

12. Haw. Rev. Stat. § 235-2.45(f)-(g), § 235-122(a)-(b), § 241-3., § 235-122

13. Idaho Code § 63-3004(a)-(b) & § 63-3030(a)(4); 2006 Form 41 Instructions-Idaho Corporation Income Tax Return, § 63-3025

14. ILCS Chapter 35 § 5/1501(a)(28), 5/201(c), 5/205(c); Ill. Adm. Code § 100.9750(c)(1)-(2).

15. Ind. Code § 6-3-2-2.8(2).

16. Iowa Code § 422.36(5), § 422.60(3)(g), § 422.60; Iowa Admin. Code § 701-52.1(5)(e).

17. Kan. Stat. Ann. § 79-32,139 & § 79-1106.

18. Ky. Rev. Stat. Ann. § 141.010(27), § 141.206(11), § 141.040(14), § 141.0401(2).

19. La. Rev. Stat. Ann. § 47:287.732(A), (B), (C), § 47:287.732.1(C).

20. Me. Rev. Stat. Ann. tit. 36, § 5102(10), § 5200, § 5206.

21. Md. Code Ann. Tax-Gen § 10-101(i), § 10-104(6), § 10-304(3); 2006 Form 510 Instructions-Pass Through Entity Income Tax Return.

22. Mass. Regs. Code § 62.17A.1(2), § 62.17A.1(1)(c)(3), § 62.17A.1(3)(b); Mass. Gen. 2 § 32D.

23. Mich. Comp. Laws § 208.31(1), § 208.35(1)(a), § 208.37; Michigan Revenue Administration Bulletin 2000-5, June 19, 2000.

24. Minn. Stat. § 290.9725 & § 290.0922(Subd. 1(b)); Minnesota Revenue Notice 98-09, June 1, 1998.

25. Miss Code Ann. § 27-8-3(1)(g), § 27-7-5(2), § 27-8-7(1), § 27-13-1(c), § 27-13-5(1), & § 27-13-7(1); Miss. Income Tax R. § 803(B), § 803(C).

26. Mo. Rev. Stat. § 143.431, § 143.471(1), § 147.010(1), § 148.620.

27. Mont. Code Ann. § 15-30-1101(1) & § 15-30-1102(1)(b)

28. Neb. Rev. Stat. § 77-2734.01(1), § 77-2734.04(3), § 77-3801(4), § 77-3802(1).

29. N.H. Rev. Stat. Ann. § 77-A:1(I), § 77-E:2, § 77-E:1(III); N.H. Admin. Rules, Rev. § 302.01(a)-(b).

30. NJ Rev. Stat. § 54:10A-5:22(a), § 54:10A-5(c)(2); N.J. Admin. Code § 18:7-20.2, § 18:7-1-18, § 18:7-11.16(a).

31. NM Stat. Ann. § 7-2A-2(G), § 7-2A-3(B); New Mexico Taxation and Revenue Dept. Ruling No. 200-01-02, June 14, 2001.

32. NY Tax Law § 208(1-A), § 210(1)(g), § 208(1-B), § 660(a)-(b).

33. NYC Admin. Code § 11-602(8)(ii); NYC Reg. § 11-27(a).

34. NC Gen. Stat. § 105-114(b)(2), § 105-122(a), § 105-130.3, § 105-131.1(a), § 105-131(b)(8), § 105-228.90(1)(b).

35. N.D. Cent. Code § 57-38-01.1, § 57-38-01.4(1).

36. Ohio Rev. Code Ann. § 5733.09(B), § 5733.01(F), § 5745.01(D); 2006 Form FT-1120 Instructions –Ohio Corporation Franchise Tax Report.

37. Okla. Stat. § 2365; Okla. Admin. Code § 710: 40-1-15.

38. Or. Rev. Stat. § 314.730(2), § 314.732(1), § 314.740, § 314.742, § 317.070, § 317.090.

39. Pa. Stat. Ann. tit. 72, § 7301(s.2), § 7301(n.1), § 7307, § 7307.9(e), § 7307.8, § 7601(2), § 7602(a), § 7602(b).

40. R.I. Gen. Laws § 44-11-2(d)(1); R.I. Reg. CT 98-13.

41. SC Code Ann. § 12-20-10(3), § 12-20-10(4), § 12-20-20(A), § 12-6-590(A) & (B), § 12-6-4430(A), § 12-6-4910(3).

42. Tenn. Code Ann. § 67-4-2006(a)(2), § 67-4-2007(e), § 67-4-2105(a).

43. Tex. Admin. Code § 3.556(b)(3), Tex. Tax Code Ann. § 171.001(a).

44. Utah Admin. R. R865.6F-34; Utah Code Ann. § 59-7-701.

45. Vt. Stat. Ann. tit. 32, § 5811(18)(B), § 5910(a)(6), 32, § 5911(a).

46. Va. Code Ann. § 58.1-401(4).

47. Wash. Rev. Code § 82.04.220, § 82.04.030.

48. W. Va. Code § 11-24-5(d), § 11-23-1, § 11-2303(b)(6).

49. Wis. Stat. § 71.34(1)-(2), § 71-35, § 71-93(1), § 71.94(1)(a).

CHAPTER FOUR

Valuing S Corporation ESOP Companies

Kathryn F. Aschwald
Donna J. Walker

On January 1, 1998, corporations with employee stock owner-ship plans (ESOPs) became eligible to elect S corporation sta-tus, and existing S corporations became eligible to form ESOPs, without nullifying the S corporation election. For 100% ESOP-owned companies, this change in the tax laws effectively eliminates federal income taxation. For companies that are less than 100% ESOP-owned, that portion of the income attributable to the ESOP's ownership is not taxable. For example, if an ESOP owns 35% of a company, then 35% of the company's income would not be taxable. The remaining 65% of the company's income would be taxable to the other shareholders at the shareholder level.

The elimination of taxes (completely for 100% ESOP-owned companies and partially for less than 100% ESOP-owned companies) presents some interesting valuation questions. Within the appraisal community, there long have been heated discussions regarding the appropriate methodologies to employ in valuing S corporations rela-tive to C corporations due to their unique tax status. Thus, to a certain degree, the question of appropriate methodologies to employ in valuing S corporation ESOPs is not a new one. However, the ESOP's ability to completely eliminate taxes in some instances introduces a new factor to be considered.

In 2001 and 2002, three U.S. Tax Court cases addressed the valuation of S corporations (*Walter L. Gross, Jr. and Barbara H. Gross, Petitioners v. Commissioner of Internal Revenue, Respondent*, T.C. Memo 1999-254; 4460-87, 4469-97; *Estate of Richie C. Heck, Petitioner v. Commissioner of Internal Revenues, Respondent*, T.C. Memo 2002-34; 11619-99; and *Estate of Wil-*

liam G. Adams, Jr. v. Commissioner of Internal Revenue, Respondent, T.C. Memo 2002-80;14698-99).[1] These cases (not specifically about ESOP S corporations) support the premise that S corporations are more valuable than identical C corporations, a premise the authors take issue with. The court cases reignited the debate that occurred in 1998 when ESOP S corporations became legal. This debate continues to the present. In these cases, the court essentially agreed with the premise that the tax benefits of an S corporation relative to a C corporation create greater value. Opponents of this view point out that this added value is only theoretical; a buyer of the S corporation would have to retain its S status to retain that benefit.

The debate concerning valuation in ESOP S corporations is more specifically focused on the income approach (valuing companies based on a discounted value of future earnings) and the valuation of minority interests (how much less buyers should pay for a less-than-control interest), particularly minority interests of companies that are making distributions significantly above those necessary to meet shareholders' tax liabilities.

The income approach issue, as we will discuss below, revolves around whether the tax shield provided by the ESOP creates additional future income compared to what would occur if the company were a C corporation. If so, how much should this additional income be counted in assessing value?

The minority interest issue is somewhat more complicated. A minority interest is generally worth less than its pro rata portion of

---

1. The latest U.S. Tax Court Case is *Robert Dallas v. Commissioner,* T.C.M. 2006-212 (2006). The tax court found for the IRS in this gift tax case. The appraisers for the taxpayer tax-affected for C corporation taxes, reasoning that the firm would most likely be sold to a C corporation. The court said it could find no evidence that the company's S corporation status was likely to be lost. It is worth noting that the court stated in *Dallas* that how ESOP S corporation stock is valued was not germane because "There is no evidence that the Department of Labor's definition of value is similar to the definition of fair market value in this case." S corporation tax affecting has also been an issue in the Delaware Court of Chancery, *Del. Open MRI Radiology Associates, P.A. v. Kessler,* 898 A.2d 290 (Del. Ch. 2006), and in at least one divorce case (the Massachusetts Supreme Judicial Court in *Judith E. Bernier v. Stephen A. Bernier,* No. SJC-09836 (Mass. Sept. 14, 2007).

the 100% equity value of the company. This is because such an interest lacks control and lacks marketability. However, if such an interest receives significant interim returns in the form of dividends, then the receipt of such income returns tends to mitigate the minority interest's lack of control and lack of marketability. Investors receiving a sufficient income return on an investment are more indifferent to their lack of control and are less concerned about the investment's lack of marketability. The investor is not dependent on selling the investment in order to realize a return. The capital gains portion of the value is less than if the company reinvested the dividends, but the income portion is greater. Such a minority interest will have lower discounts for lack of control and lack of marketability, and thus, its fair market value may be much closer to its pro rata portion of the company's 100% equity value then a similar minority interest not receiving dividends or receiving dividends sufficient only to meet the owner's tax obligations. The fair market value of such a minority interest will never equal its pro rata portion of the 100% value, because the interest does not have the ability to declare dividends. Therefore, it is at risk that dividends may be reduced or completely curtailed.

The decisions rendered in the tax court cases cited above involve facts and circumstances unique to the specific companies. A discussion of the court cases is not germane to this chapter, and in the opinion of the authors the court cases are not applicable to S corporation ESOP valuation in general.

Impact of S Corporation Election on ESOP Company Cash Flows

Less Than 100% ESOP

In this case, the cash savings to the company are limited because cash payments are generally made to all shareholders so that the non-ESOP shareholders have cash available to pay taxes on the S corporation income attributable to the non-ESOP shareholders at the shareholder level. The distributions made to meet these personal tax obligations go, in the case of the non-ESOP shareholders, directly to the shareholder, and, in the case of the ESOP, to the ESOP trust. In either case, the cash is no longer available to the company to reinvest into productive assets. To the extent that these distributions can be used by the ESOP to pay principal and interest (in the case of a leveraged ESOP) or to pay ESOP benefit distributions, then there is a cash savings to the extent that distributions result in lower company contributions to the ESOP.

100% ESOP

In an S corporation that is 100% owned by an ESOP, there are no corporate federal income (and often state) taxes paid. Therefore, the company realizes, on an annual basis, a cash savings equal to the dollar amount of the taxes the company would have to pay were it a C corporation.

Appraisal Methodologies

The Internal Revenue Service (IRS) and the U.S. Department of Labor (DOL) generally govern appraisals for ESOP purposes. In this chapter, we will not discuss appraisal methodologies as they apply to ESOPs in general, but rather how they apply to ESOP S corporations specifically.

Value Enhancement Associated with
S Corporation Election

There is no question that the absence of taxes represents true cash savings to a company. It follows, then, that the cash savings should translate into some form of enhanced value.

From the most global perspective, value is enhanced via the increase in cash flows available to the company. The source of these cash flows is the cash that would otherwise have gone to pay corporate federal income taxes. As discussed above, the magnitude of the savings depends on the percentage of the company owned by the ESOP. This value enhancement is realized in one of two ways: either through reinvestment of cash flows or through the payment of regular dividends. The reinvestment of the added cash flows into productive assets earning a return in excess of the company's cost of capital enhances value over time as those assets become productive and generate additional cash flows and higher levels of growth than would otherwise be the case. When the cash flows are paid out in the form of dividends, the owner of the ESOP common stock earns a portion of its total return in the form of dividends. In this case, the value is captured either in a capitalization of dividends approach or in the increased marketability (or conversely lower marketability discount) of the security due to its higher income return. The capital gains portion of the value is less than if the company reinvested the added cash flows, but the income portion is higher.

If the company merely retains the added cash flows in the form of cash and marketable securities, which do not earn a return in excess of the company's cost of capital, the S corporation election may not be value enhancing. *The mere avoidance of taxes does not enhance value. The cash savings associated with the S corporation status must be put to productive use.*

Initial Transactions and Updates

Standard of Value. A significant governing factor in considering the most appropriate appraisal methodologies is the standard of value for ESOP appraisals. IRS regulations, proposed regulations by the DOL, and general case law dictate that the appropriate standard of value is fair market value. Fair market value is defined as follows:

> Fair market value is considered to represent a value at which a willing seller and willing buyer, both being informed of the relevant facts about the business, could reasonably conduct a transaction, neither person acting under compulsion to do so.

Appropriate Methodologies Within the Context of Fair Market Value. The appropriate standard of value and the definition of fair market value require an appraisal incorporating the concept of "any willing buyer" and "any willing seller." For the ESOP company to retain its S election (and the associated tax savings), it must be purchased by an S corporation. The presumption of an S corporation buyer violates the fair market value standard because another S corporation is a specific buyer. It follows, then, that for annual update and transaction purposes, the S corporation is appropriately valued as if it were a C corporation.

Given that valuing the S corporation ESOP company as a C corporation is appropriate, it is not appropriate to do the following:

1. Apply after-tax multiples to pretax numbers.
2. Add the present value of the tax savings associated with the S corporation election.
3. Apply after-tax discount rates to pretax cash flows.

It is extremely important to recognize, however, that this does not mean that there will not be added value associated with the S corporation status. The value of the S corporation election is realized over time as the cash flows are reinvested and the company's earnings are higher and/or growing faster than if the company were a C corporation. Intuitively this makes sense. "Any willing buyer" would naturally pay for value enhancements resulting from the reinvestment of cash flows into income-producing assets that were already in place earning a return. Those value enhancements or assets are transferable to "any willing buyer." It also follows, then, that there is no immediate "value pick-up" associated with S corporation status.

As a result, in an initial transaction, the ESOP should generally not pay for value enhancements that are not already in place. Nor should an ESOP pay for benefits that it brings to the table (such as the S election). As discussed above, when the added cash flows are paid out in the form of dividends, the enhanced value is captured in the increased liquidity (and thus the application of a lower discount for lack of marketability) associated with closely held paying securities.

To the extent large cash balances are developed over time, value may even be enhanced from an acquisition standpoint for those ESOP S corporations that simply hold their added cash flows. It is not likely that this value transfers to a minority shareholder, and to the extent it does transfer, it certainly is less than dollar-for-dollar.

Some argue that there is a significant amount of economic value associated with the S corporation election for ESOP companies, and that this economic value is equal to the present value of (or a multiple of) the future tax savings as a result of the S corporation election. Again, however, one must recognize that to retain this economic value, another S corporation must purchase the company and maintain the ESOP to keep the tax savings. Because there are far fewer S corporations than C corporations, the likelihood of an available S corporation buyer is much less. Therefore, within the context of fair market value, the presumption of an S corporation buyer requires the assumption of severely reduced liquidity resulting from a reduced number of "willing buyers." This reduced liquidity and resulting higher discount for lack of marketability would offset the added value implied by the present value of the tax savings to a large (if not total) extent. In addition, many other taxes (such as the LIFO recapture tax, and the built-in capital gains tax, which will be discussed later) may in fact be due from an S corporation upon sale of the company and/or upon conversion to an S corporation. These taxes would offset any value attributable to the tax savings calculated in this way.

Taking this concept one step further, one merely needs to consider the theory from a market perspective. Valuing the tax savings implicitly as described above presumes that a buyer of the S corporation would apply a multiple to pretax income. Assuming a 40% tax rate, a multiple of 5, and $100 pretax income, this implies a significantly higher price for the S corporation, as shown in table 4-1.

Table 4-1. Applying a Multiple to Pretax Income

	S Corporation	C Corporation
Pretax income	$100	$100
Corporate taxes	$ 0	$ 40
Net income	$100	$ 60
Times 5.0 multiple	x 5	x 5
Value	$500	$300

The question is, would any "willing buyer" (or any buyer) pay 67% more ($500 versus $300) for an S corporation relative to a C corporation? We believe the answer to this question is no. To a C corporation buyer, the S status of the selling company would be of no value. If the buyer were an individual, it would be more economical for that buyer to buy a C corporation and convert it to an S corporation. The cost of doing so would be much less that 67% greater price for the S corporation. Such an individual may be willing to pay a premium for an S corporation but no more than the cost of converting a C corporation to an S corporation. If the buyer were an existing S corporation, it would not pay for tax benefits it already had.

Sale of Company and/or ESOP Termination

We stated above that in an initial transaction, the ESOP should not pay for value enhancements that are not already in place, nor should it pay for benefits that it brings to the table such as the tax-free status in a S election. However, when the ESOP is selling its position, it may be appropriate for the ESOP trustee to consider the favorable S corporation tax treatment.

When an ESOP is selling its position or being terminated, the standard of value is still fair market value. However, the financial advisor to the ESOP trustee is often asked to determine whether the transaction is fair to the ESOP from a financial point of view. This is generally interpreted to mean that the transaction must be fair to the ESOP in both absolute terms (not less than fair market value) and relative terms when compared to many financial factors that are not necessarily part of fair market value. For example, is the consideration being received by the ESOP the same as other transaction participants? If the ESOP is leveraged with debt outstanding, we look to see whether or not the ESOP's return on investment would be higher if it did not sell and simply held its investment until the debt was paid down. When the ESOP is considering a sale of its interest, then the trustee must determine that the sale is in the best interests of the ESOP participants. Therefore, a careful analysis of financial factors in addition to fair market value may include an analysis of the enhanced cash flow enjoyed by an S corporation ESOP. This is referred to by some as the ESOP's "economic value." It is typically defined as the present value of the ESOP's pro rata portion of expected corporate income tax savings under an S election discounted at an equity-required rate of return. Many assume that fair market value will be below economic value.

The question is then whether the ESOP can sell at fair market value and thus below economic value. Arguably, an ESOP trustee would have difficulty accepting a fair market value buyout price if the economic value was considerably higher and no compelling reasons for a sale existed. This is most likely with a 100% ESOP-owned S corporation. In other words, an ESOP owning 100% of an S corporation may have a hold position, due to cash flows that are 100% free of corporate income taxes, that is more valuable than the price that a financial buyer or even a strategic buyer may be willing to pay. Absent compelling factors such as poor or deteriorating industry conditions or a repurchase obligation outstripping the liquidity abilities of the company, there may be no reason for the ESOP to forego its enhanced expected future cash flows if its return on investment is higher under a hold position than if it sells its ownership position. In terms of financial fairness, this seems entirely appropriate. It would be unfair to the ESOP to sell if it resulted in a return on investment below the return available to participants if the company continued on a stand-alone basis.

However, the discrepancy between fair market value and economic value as described above may be greatly overstated. First, the calculation of economic value must include all tax impacts. There are costs to converting to an S corporation as well as tax savings. These include LIFO recapture taxes and costs relating to the write-off of deferred tax assets and liabilities. Based on the experience of some of our ESOP clients who have converted from C to S corporate status, the break-even period may be two to three years. In addition, S corporations may be taxed on excessive passive income (over 25% of revenues) carried over from prior C corporation status, Finally, S corporations are subject to a built-in gains tax on disposition of appreciated property carried over from the prior C corporation. This can be significant, particularly in the case where the value of the company experiences rapid growth from the time of conversion from C to S status. Also, some consideration must be given to possible changes in tax laws that eliminate the tax advantages of S corporations.

These costs may (most likely in the first years after the conversion), when factored in with the tax savings, reduce "economic value" and the relative difference to fair market value. Assuming over time the productive deployment of enhanced cash flows, the value of the S corporation will increase. As stated above, a third party should be willing to pay for this value because it is reflective of productive assets, not a tax status, and because it is transferable to a third party. Thus, over time, fair market value and economic value should converge, and "economic value" should be reflected in the price offered by a prospective buyer.

In conclusion, we urge caution in analyzing the concept of "economic value" as it pertains to S corporation ESOPs. While there may be some intuitive appeal to the concept, economic value is difficult to determine because it is affected by many variables:

- The level of distributions
- Subsequent investment returns
- Expected tax rates in the future
- Expected holding period of investment
- Expected sale price of investments at the end of the hold period

At a minimum, it must be considered within the context of the factors discussed above that offset economic value, such as the built-in capital gains tax.

In any transaction, from a fairness perspective, the question of whether or not the shareholder is being adequately compensated for his or her investment, given the terms of the transaction, is addressed. The 100% ESOP S corporation situation is no different. From this viewpoint, the analysis becomes a hold-versus-sell decision. As such, factors to be considered include a comparison of fair market value as a going concern compared to the proposed transaction price, the expected return if the ESOP holds its investment, the expected return if the ESOP sells its investment, and the risk factors that would tend to offset economic value.

Conclusion

No increase in value is appropriate in the appraisal of S corporation ESOPs only as a result of a change in tax status. It is not appropriate to add the present value of the tax benefits. The appropriate standard of value and the definition of fair market value require an appraisal incorporating the concept of "any willing buyer" and "any willing seller." For the ESOP company to retain its S election (and the associated tax savings), it must be purchased by an S corporation or individuals eligible to elect S corporate status. The presumption of an S corporation buyer violates the fair market value standard because another S corporation is a specific buyer. It follows, then, that for annual update and transaction purposes, the S corporation is appropriately valued as if it were a C corporation. The ESOP generally should not pay for the S corporation status at an initial transaction or for update purposes. However, consideration of the enhanced cash flows resulting from the S corporation status that have not yet been invested into productive assets may be appropriate as a part of the consideration of overall fairness when the ESOP is selling its ownership position or being terminated.

-

CHAPTER FIVE

Administrative and Operational Issues Resulting from the S Election

Anthony I. Mathews

There is no question that the ESOP-owned S corporation is the most amazing and tax-effective structure ever conceived in U.S. tax law. It potentially gives ESOP companies a significant advantage over non-ESOP-owned companies based solely on their being broadly owned by their employees. Following the adoption of the original legislation that authorized the S corporation ESOP, the flood of potentially abusive applications of the concept led to a robust response from the government, which in turn resulted in a very stable legal and regulatory platform from which to operate these plans. In effect, the anti-abuse legislation has solidified this advantage for companies that are true to the vision of broad-based employee ownership.

In light of the advantages of this structure, administrative difficulties seem almost insignificant, but it is only fair to say that there are a number of difficulties associated with operating an ESOP-owned S corporation that should be considered in the context of making the election. The purpose of this chapter is to highlight a number of primarily administrative matters that are likely to require focus, discussion, and resolution following the change to S corporation status as well as to discuss some unorthodox applications of the administrative process that might offer even more extraordinary benefits from this configuration.

Extraordinary administrative complexity in this configuration comes from the interaction of several features of general ESOP law with several features of S corporation law as well as features of special

ESOP S corporation law designed to curb abuses of the form. Any time you get three sets of laws involved, things get complicated.

In general, complexities arise from the fact that S corporations:

- Pay no (or little) tax directly on their earnings. S corporation shareholders are personally taxed on their ratable portion of the corporation's earnings, based on their percentage of ownership throughout the year.

- Routinely (although not necessarily) distribute earnings to share-holders in amounts at least sufficient to allow shareholders to pay their taxes.

- Have restrictions on the number of shareholders they may have at any point in time.

- May not have their stock held by certain types of entities.

- May generally only issue a single class of stock.

In contrast, ESOP companies:

- Generally want to retain value for current employees.

- Tend to try to manage cash flow by deferring distributions of value to terminated participants.

- Often use dividends to supplement contributions in order to amortize ESOP loans or create current cash incentives for participants.

- Have often used separate classes of stock in order to focus the effect of dividends.

- Are frequently created to provide significant tax benefits (to sellers and corporate sponsors) through the rollover and deferral of gain on sales to the plan and by making use of extraordinary tax deduction limits.

And Congress has adopted special rules to:

- Assure that S corporation ESOPs actually benefit a broad cross-section of employees (even more so than the rules that apply to all qualified retirement plans).

- Limit the applicability of other extraordinary tax benefits beyond the basic ability to have corporate taxable income attributed to a tax-exempt entity.

The purpose of this chapter is to discuss some of the major operational issues that arise from the interaction of these features. And, although all these issues are interactions of multiple factors, we'll try to cluster them together into operating concepts.

S Corporations May Issue Only a Single Class of Stock

One major change to ongoing ESOP allocations arises as a result of the fact that an S corporation may only issue a single class of stock, and ESOP companies have often created systems to allow for the treatment of ESOP shares to differ from the treatment of other non-ESOP-owned shares. Where certain shares are treated materially differently than others, the IRS can declare that that different treatment constitutes a separate class of stock (regardless of the technical fact of the matter), and your S election can be voided.

This tends to show up where an ESOP company is applying dividends as a way of funding the ESOP either to supplement contributions for loan payment purposes or to pass through to participants as a current cash incentive. C corporation ESOPs can deduct dividends paid on ESOP shares when the dividends are used to repay an ESOP loan (dividends are also deductible in C corporation ESOPs if they are passed through to employees and/or employees voluntarily reinvest them in company stock). Dividends used to repay an ESOP loan in a C corporation also do not count against contribution limits. That has often meant that in C corporations, a separate class of ESOP stock is created (or that other shareholders waive their right to dividends) so that dividends can be focused only where needed to assist funding. Used in that manner, C corporation dividends have become a reliable way of supplementing employer contributions to repay ESOP debt or creating additional tax deductions through the pass-through. And, acknowledging this, Congress has carved out a set of provisions in the Internal Revenue Code (the "Code") designed to control how C corporation dividends are used in order to insure that ESOP participants receive fair value for any dividends they might receive.

When you convert to S corporation status, all of those practices change materially. Since an S corporation may issue only one class of stock, any special focusing of dividends to special ESOP shares will not be possible without risking the election itself. Any distribution of earnings (the equivalent of a dividend in a C corporation) must be distributed evenly to all shares of issued and outstanding stock and to all shareholders. Favoring one shareholder over another can be interpreted to be creating that separate class of stock (with a preference for dividends), and that would void the S election.

This fact cuts both ways. It is not possible to focus the application of dividends (distributions) only on ESOP shares, so if you are planning to use them to supplement contributions for ESOP funding, you will have to gross up the distributions to cover all shareholders ratably. At the same time, where it is the practice of S corporations to distribute earnings to shareholders to, at least, cover their tax liability, the ESOP must be in line to receive its share of distributions as well. In either case, there may be a larger commitment of cash to the process than was the case under the C corporation rules.

Leveraged ESOP Accounting and Allocation Rules

Code Section 404(k) provided C corporations with a number of elaborate mechanisms and tests for applying dividends to fund the ESOP. Because dividends are not subject to the limitations applicable to contributions, this provision provided a very efficient way to maximize the purchasing power of an ESOP. In its original form, this section specifically excluded S corporations from those mechanisms, the result of which was to limit the amount of earnings distributions applied to repay debt to those applicable to unallocated shares only (i.e., only the earnings on the collateral, as provided in the original prohibited transaction exemption). In 2004, the American Jobs Creation Act corrected the disparity between C corporations and S corporations in this important area. Under current rules, the treatment of S corporation earnings distributions is governed by the same rules as those applicable to C corporations. That is, earnings on previously allocated shares may be used to make payments on the loan used to acquire those shares, provided the value added to participants' accounts as a result of using those earnings is at least equal to the earnings that were used.

In either case, earnings distributions paid on unallocated shares and used to repay an ESOP loan can be allocated to employee accounts based on the company's contribution formula or on the basis of relative account balances. Distributions paid on allocated shares must be allocated based on relative stock account balances.

S Corporation Earnings Flow Through and Are Taxed Directly to the Shareholders

The major attraction of the S election has always been the notion of a single level of tax. S corporations pay no taxes directly (or small taxes, depending on state laws). Their shareholders pay taxes directly based on their relative shareholdings. This is, in fact, the basis of the miracle of the S corporation ESOP—since the ESOP is a tax-exempt trust fund, its share of earnings is effectively non-taxable.

As a result of their shareholders' direct tax liability, S corporations generally pay out to shareholders a distribution of S corporation earnings at least sufficient to cover their state and federal income taxes. As a practical matter, since all shareholders must be treated identically, this means an amount equal to the highest marginal tax rate applicable to any of the shareholders. (Depending on the state where the shareholder resides, this rate can be as high as 45%.) Where the non-ESOP shareholders own small percentages of the total and are also employees of the company, it may be possible to create a bonus for them (grossed up, perhaps to cover the gap between pretax bonuses and after-tax earnings distributions) that coincidentally is sufficient to meet their tax liability without making such a distribution. These would, of course, be subject to reasonable compensation considerations and other issues, but in some cases it might do the job.

In most cases, however, where an ESOP owns less than 100% of the outstanding stock, the corporation will likely be inclined to declare and pay such earnings distributions to the non-ESOP shareholders, and a pro-rata earnings distribution will be required on the ESOP shares as well. The payment of this distribution can result in some interesting and potentially challenging benefits issues.

As noted earlier, earnings distributions on allocated shares (whether dividends or distributions) are generally allocated to participant accounts on the basis of the stock balances that generated them. Company contributions, on the other hand, are generally allocated based on compensation. As noted, the effect of these differing bases on allocations can be profound in that allocations based on stock account balances will generally favor the longer-term, more highly compensated employees who have the largest balances, and allocations based on compensation will generally have less of an inclination in that direction. With regard to earnings distributions on stock that has not yet been allocated, the plan has the ability to determine where those will flow. Plan designs may call for such distributions to be allocated as if they were contributions (i.e. on the basis of salaries) or as if they were earnings (i.e. on the basis of account balances—either stock only or total) or some other formula that is nondiscriminatory.

Despite these constraints, there is significant flexibility in managing the flow of earnings into ESOP accounts in an S corporation, and planning in advance is critical.

For an extreme example, assume that the K Company is an S corporation that adopted a leveraged ESOP to effect a leveraged ESOP purchase of 100% of the company. Let us say further that the K Company management has decided to make a single contribution in the first year to get the ball rolling and then to fund the plan entirely with earnings distributions from then on. If the plan calls for those earnings distributions to be allocated based on stock account balances, only the participants there for the first allocation will ever get any stock. There are other restrictions on the use of S corporation earnings to pay debt that would make that mathematically difficult to accomplish, and it is likely that the practice would cause prohibited discrimination, but it is theoretically possible to create that outcome. That means that an S corporation ESOP plan sponsor has the ability to design outcomes to a greater extent than C corporation counterparts.

In the case of an ESOP that owns 100% of the outstanding stock, there is no compulsion to pay out any earnings distribution (since the ESOP taxpayer's marginal tax rate is 0%). The decision whether to pay such distribution on the ESOP shares, then, can be seen as generally an employee benefit decision or it can be driven by the ESOP's loan funding requirements.

In any case, these earnings distributions provide some material planning opportunities, especially as they represent a mechanism for providing significant funding to the plan that is *not* counted as an annual addition for the purpose of the Code Section 415 allocation limits.

Voting ESOP Shares

Although an S corporation is permitted to have a class of voting stock and a class of nonvoting common stock, the ESOP must hold the shares of the voting class if the ESOP is to meet the requirement that it be designed to invest in "qualifying employer securities" that are defined as those having the highest combination of dividend and voting rights. A class of convertible preferred or super-common stock that is often used in C corporation leveraged ESOP transactions would not be permissible.

Issues Related to the Number and Eligibility of Shareholders

S corporations are currently required to limit the number of shareholders to 100. All shareholders must be individuals (or equivalents) who are U.S. residents for tax purposes. The ESOP counts as a single shareholder, but when participants receive shares, their ownership counts individually. The status of a corporation as an S corporation may be inadvertently terminated if the corporation has more than 100 shareholders on any day or if stock is transferred to an ineligible shareholder. Corporations, partnerships, certain types of trusts, Individual Retirement Accounts (IRAs) (generally), and nonresident aliens are ineligible shareholders.

In light of all of these considerations, the Code was amended to provide that an S corporation need not offer terminated participants the right to demand distribution in the form of stock provided it is ready to make distributions in the form of cash. Please note that it is not a requirement that S corporations pay out benefits in cash only (as I have heard more than once), but it is an exception to the rule that generally requires ESOPs and stock bonus plans to allow for the distribution of benefits in the form of employer stock. This exception, like that available to corporations with a bylaw restriction on stock ownership, is included in most plan documents in order to help manage these requirements and protect the S status, but, as certain benefits to both ESOP sponsors and participants derive from making stock distributions, it may be of interest to the company to find other ways to get there.

In any case, these ownership restrictions give rise to significant changes in many plan operation policies as companies convert from C to S status.

In C corporations, it has been a common practice to establish benefit distribution procedures that take the form of a distribution of whole shares of company stock that can be transferred or rolled over to an IRA or can be sold back to the company under the required put option. Often this "stock distribution" technique is used to accomplish a distribution and installment repurchase (both fixing the cost of a payout and, at the same time, deferring its cost) where the distribution is followed by an exercise by the participant or an IRA trustee of the participant's put option, which the company honors by either a cash payment or a secured promissory note. From the terminated participant's point of view, a stock distribution may offer the best tax outcome possible. Under current rules, where a participant takes a lump-sum distribution of stock from an ESOP and then sells the stock at some later point it is possible to elect to have the trust's cost basis taxed as ordinary income and the net unrealized appreciation taxed as long-term capital gains no matter how the employee has held the stock at the time it is sold. On larger distributions, this can represent a substantial savings for the participant. Please note that for this purpose, a "lump-sum" distribution has a very specific meaning—the balance to an employee's credit from the plan in a single tax year as a result of termination that results in a break in service. A rollover to an IRA or other plan (even if the distribution is in stock itself) eliminates this benefit.

In short, stock distributions can be instrumental in creating both favorable cash management for the company and the best tax outcome for the participant. In an S corporation, this pattern could seriously risk the S election because IRAs are generally not qualified S corporation shareholders, and distributing shares to individuals raises the risk of either having too many shareholders or inadvertently transferring shares to some other nonqualified shareholder.

The original ESOP S corporation legislation, the Taxpayer Relief Act of 1997 ("TRA 97"), provided partial relief from an unintended possible termination of the S corporation due to a large number of terminated ESOP participants electing to receive distributions in the form of shares of stock by exempting S corporations from the requirement to offer stock as a distribution form provided distributions are available in cash. Code Section 409(h)(2) provides that an ESOP maintained by an S corporation may make distributions in cash without entitling participants to elect a distribution in the form of shares of stock.

In a 2001 Private Letter Ruling, the IRS resolved the IRA difficulty for a specific taxpayer by finding that momentary ownership of shares by an IRA would not jeopardize the S corporation status provided that the shares were only held by the IRA briefly (on a single day) and were immediately repurchased under a formal plan of the employer requiring their immediate repurchase. With Rev. Rul. 2003-23, the IRS favorably resolved this issue for all S corporation ESOPs and expanded the scope of the rule to clearly allow for the repurchase of distributed shares to be made in the form of a promissory note (although there still remain significant issues related to proper collateral for these notes).

There remains, however, the overall restriction on the number of shareholders that may exist in an S corporation (currently 100), so if you are thinking of beginning or continuing stock distributions from your S corporation ESOP, you will have to be very careful not to inadvertently revoke the election by violating any of these rules.

S Corporations Are Generally Required to Operate on a Calendar Tax Year

Except where the principal shareholders pay taxes on an other-than-calendar-year basis or where there is a significant business reason to maintain a non-calendar year, S corporations are generally required to operate on a calendar tax year. So, in the normal course of events, a corporation that is currently on a fiscal year may not be allowed to continue on that basis after an election to be taxed as an S corporation.

Where an ESOP is purchasing stock such that it will own 100% of the company and where the ESOP's plan year is a fiscal year, the company may continue to treat the ESOP plan year as its fiscal year as a result of the majority shareholder exception to the requirement. Where the ESOP owns less than 100% of the shares of the company, however, IRS has indicated that it will ignore the ESOP's ownership for this purpose and determine the required tax year with regard only to the other shareholders and the business reason test. In order to retain a non-calendar fiscal year in that context, then, a company will need to demonstrate a business reason for the accounting period.

Where the company is changing its tax year at the same time it is making the election to be taxed as an S corporation, according to IRS publications, it will not automatically be allowed to make the election to switch for a period immediately following a short fiscal period. Instead, it may have to wait until the beginning of the next fiscal period following a 12-month fiscal period and convert to S corporation status at that time. The IRS has the authority to grant individual relief on this point, and it has done so on many occasions so far.

The major issues that emerge from the change in fiscal year have to do with the operational results of short periods in qualified plans. Where a plan year changes, the plan must provide that no participant's benefit will, in any way, be reduced solely by virtue of the change. This means that you will either have to continue to track all the benefit-related processes on both the old year basis and the new year basis, awarding the highest generated benefits to every participant, or, as is most often the case, to award credit for the short period on some basis that puts everyone ahead of where they would have been on the original basis. As a practical matter, this generally results in increases in vesting and other benefit accruals that can be quite expensive if you are tracking your liability. This cost should very definitely be included in the analysis of the change, and it is often overlooked.

In the end, this can generally be resolved by simply leaving the ESOP plan year on a fiscal basis not synchronized with your corporate fiscal year. Although this does fix the "unexpected additional benefit" issue, it also creates issues related to the timing of deductions and other mechanical matters.

Like everything, this is an area of trade-offs that should be thoroughly quantified before the election is finalized.

Issues Related to Trying to Get the Best of Both Worlds

The most significant benefits for sellers in ESOP transactions accrue in the C corporation format, while the most significant tax benefits for companies on an ongoing basis accrue in the S corporation format. For that reason, it is often an objective to accomplish an ESOP transaction while a C corporation and then elect to be an S corporation immediately after the transaction. Where a company is a C corporation in the first place, other than the accounting rules that govern the election to be an S corporation, there is no reason this cannot be accomplished, but that "other than" is usually a pretty big one. Converting from C to S corporation status will cause changes in accounting for the corporation that may affect the decision. S corporations must account for their taxes on a full accrual basis. Likewise, inventory must be counted on a LIFO basis, and other changes must be implemented. The first stop on the decision tree here will be with the CPAs to determine what the exact cost of the conversion will be. The second stop will be with your appraiser to determine the value of all your assets on the date the election is made so that if you later sell any of those items, the BIG (built-in gains) tax will be payable only on the portion of any gain that existed at the time of the conversion.

Generally, though, these matters are not persuasive in either direction, and the pattern of completing transactions as a C corporation and then converting to S when the tax benefits are greatest is very common.

If a corporation has made an election to be treated as an S corporation and subsequently elects to terminate the S corporation status (in order, for example, to accomplish an ESOP transaction that will qualify the seller for deferral of the taxable gain), the corporation (and any successor corporation) will not be eligible to make an S corporation election again for a period of five years. What this generally means is that ESOP transactions in this situation should be designed to provide significant tax benefits through deductible contributions for the first five years after the transaction; then, the S corporation election can be renewed.

Undistributed Earnings Adjust the Cost Basis of S Corporation Shares

To the extent earnings of an S corporation are not currently distributed to shareholders, there is an entry in the S corporation's financials called an accumulated adjustments account. Unlike C corporation retained earnings (the equivalent to the accumulated adjustments account), these accumulated amounts create an adjustment (increase) in the shareholders' cost basis in their shares (see Revenue Ruling 2003-27).

One significant benefit available to ESOP participants may be eliminated in planning around other S corporation issues. As mentioned earlier, under current rules, a participant may have the ability to elect long-term capital gain treatment on the net unrealized appreciation included in a distribution of ESOP stock. Over time, this benefit will be compromised by the accumulated adjustments as corporate earnings are not distributed to the ESOP and the cost basis of the ESOP trust is increased accordingly. In most cases, having the cost basis increased improves the tax outcome, but in this case, it means that a larger portion of the distribution will be taxed as ordinary income and a smaller portion is potentially taxed as a capital gain. Of course, this benefit will be eliminated altogether if the plan elects to forbid stock distributions altogether.

The exact methodology for applying the cost basis adjustment is not entirely clear—whether to apply the adjustment across all accounts ratably or to apply a plan-level cost basis number to all shares is not clear.

Other Potential Issues Related to Benefit Distribution Practices

In general, especially where S corporation earnings distributions are intended to play a significant role in ESOP funding, competition will develop between the desire not to create an incentive for participants to quit employment early to get at their ESOP benefit accumulation and the desire to keep as much of the earnings distribution as possible for the benefit of current employees. And ESOP benefit distribution policies are often crafted as a compromise between retaining corporate cash flow to every extent possible versus restricting the benefits of stock ownership to current employees (or, looked at another equally justified way, protecting terminees from the involuntary risk of an undiversified, illiquid investment).

Trying to compromise those objectives is by far the most difficult of the planning challenges faced by ESOP sponsors in the conversion from C to S corporation tax status. For example, the desire to restrict earnings distributions to current employees can be properly implemented only by cashing out terminees as rapidly as possible from their stock balances. This will obviously cause significant short-term cash requirements in either making rapid benefit distributions to terminees or, if you want to also avoid creating a significant incentive to quit caused by rapid benefit distributions from the plan, in creating segregated accounts for terminees that are not invested in employer stock but are still held for a future distribution. You get the idea. It is a constantly moving target, and there is no perfect compromise.

On a related matter, where an S corporation elects to redeem terminated participants' stock and retire it rather than recycle it within the plan, distributions will have to be made in the form of stock subject to an immediate (perhaps even automatic) sale to the company through the put option. Otherwise, the transaction will be one that requires an updated appraisal as of the date of the redemption because it is a transaction between the plan and the company rather than a benefit distribution.

Also, the "sale exemption" of ERISA Section 408(e), permitting purchases and sales of qualifying employer securities between a plan and a party in interest, may not be available to a person who is an owner-employee of an S corporation (basically anyone who owns more than 50% of its stock). The Taxpayer Relief Act of 1997 amended this provision to permit an ESOP to purchase stock from such an employer-employee or an S corporation, but it was not amended to clearly exempt the sale of shares from the ESOP to the company. This may be an issue if the benefit distribution policy implemented by the company requires a redemption of shares by the company directly from the ESOP.

Code Section 409(o) allows an ESOP sponsor to defer distributions of leveraged ESOP shares through the term of an ESOP loan. The method for identifying shares that may take advantage of this deferral involves a reference to Section 404(a)(9), which specifically refers to C corporations. It is not 100% clear that this ability, then, is available to S corporations, so if you want to use it, the best course of action is to put in your plan document that you intend to defer such distributions and get a determination letter that says it is OK.

Special ESOP Anti-Abuse Testing Issues

Considering how utterly wonderful the tax benefits of the S corporation ESOP are, it is no surprise that immediately upon passage of the enabling legislation, the blue-suit contingent began feverishly searching for ways to pervert its intent—that is to create all the tax benefits of the S corporation ESOP for a small group of executives or former owners without actually sharing any material ownership at all. The schemes that were developed to do this range from simple approaches like just incorporating a one- or two-person business as an ESOP-owned S corporation (with the one or two persons playing the part of employees, participants, selling shareholders, and everything else) to more complex approaches using things like management company structures to funnel all the value out of an ESOP company into the hands of executives while retaining all the tax benefits. Whatever the form, the result of these schemes was the same—they purport to create the tax benefits of the ESOP-owned S corporation without really sharing ownership. As they got more notoriety, there was a real risk that these shenanigans might have jeopardized the ESOP S corporation altogether.

Instead, as a result of significant lobbying efforts on the part of the ESOP community, in 2001, EGTRRA (the Economic Growth and Tax Relief Reconciliation Act) added to law a group of provisions designed to prevent the abuses from occurring without disabling legitimate applications. Code Section 409(p) contains these provisions, and while they seem simple enough in concept, they contain many complexities in their implementation. Regulations adopted under Section 409(p) clarified and added specific guidance to the provisions, and, though there are still some areas of continued concern, the tests are definitely workable. Although a separate chapter in this book discusses the mechanics of the tests, it may be worthwhile to talk a bit about the operational specifics that may change your life.

Basically, the thrust of the rules is to prohibit the concentration of ownership of an ESOP-owned S corporation in the hands of a few individuals. That is, it is the clear intention of Congress that the significant benefit attached to being an ESOP-owned S corporation will be available only where there is a broad distribution of the ownership. Seems simple enough?

Section 409(p) accomplishes this by creating the concept of "disqualified persons" and declaring a "nonallocation year" for any plan year during which the disqualified persons hold more than a threshold percentage of ownership of the company. The Code then goes on to levy significant penalties against the accounts and accumulations of disqualified persons in the ESOP. These penalties are material enough that, in the main, a company would be better off forgoing the S corporation status than paying the penalties. And that, after all is said and done, is the real result of violating these rules—the offending company is essentially forced to operate as a C corporation.

It seems straightforward enough, but as always, the devil is in the details. Here are a few of those bedeviled details:

- Since all the references to "disqualified persons" take into account the broad family group, you may have to begin tracking family relationships that you have not had to track before.

- You are definitely going to have to begin to include in your ESOP administration all sorts of nonqualified plan information (stock options, long-term deferred compensation, and other "quasi-equity" instruments) that you have never had to include before. You may even have to invade confidential executive compensation agreements to assemble the information you need to perform the tests.

- Since all ESOP shares are considered "deemed-owned" shares, you'll have to add another allocation step to create the share balance that is attributed to all ESOP participants (their ratable portion of the unallocated suspense shares) in order to do the tests.

- This section adds yet another test that must be done to confirm the compliance of an ESOP, but unlike other tests that may be done following the end of a plan year, this test should be done prospectively as soon as it can be done to assure that the plan is in compliance at all times since the penalties will accrue if you are an S corporation in violation of these restrictions at any time.

- After all is said and done, though, probably the most difficult of the tasks confronting the administrator of this test is keeping track of all the attribution chains and determining exactly what constitutes deemed-owned shares. Clearly, your ESOP administrator will have to be given a considerable amount of information that might not otherwise be necessary, including information on all your executive incentive plans (including deferred compensation as well as any equity-based incentive programs).

It looks like most (although not all) legitimate applications of the ESOP S corporation structure (at least ones we could all probably agree are legitimate) will be able to fly with these rules. It seems especially problematic for smaller companies that might have accruals within the ESOP that could run afoul of these rules.

If it looks like you might have trouble passing the Section 409(p) tests, there are several approaches that may help you solve the problem. IRS guidance (in the form of the final regulations) lists a number of approaches to resolving these risks. In general, these fixes are ways to restrict the accumulation of deemed-owned shares so as to avoid creating disqualified persons. And in this arena, the fewer disqualified persons, the better. In fact, some plans are simply excluding any disqualified person from the ESOP altogether. Be careful with this approach, though. In the first year the rules apply, the penalty is on the total balance of any disqualified persons, so just excluding them may not eliminate the penalty. You'll also have to be careful about using other nonqualified benefits as a way to compensate them for their losses because those nonqualified benefits are also deemed-owned shares and can just make the matter worse.

It is probably a better approach to simply limit the allocations to disqualified persons as a matter of the formulas in the plan. This should not be discriminatory (in a way that is prohibited, in any case), and it can be made to work. But be careful: the requirements exist on each day of the year. And it is very possible to create disqualified persons inadvertently by doing something quite unrelated to the ESOP (at least in your thinking), and the penalties are very punitive.

There are a number of other milder approaches to managing this. It may also be possible, for example, to reshuffle balances in a plan that has substantial cash balances in addition to the stock so that the stock is more evenly distributed. It may also be possible to introduce more people and more equity into the process so that the concentration of ownership is diluted. This could come from merging with another company so that the percentage interest of the individuals never reaches the 10% level.

If all else fails, the regulations make clear that it is acceptable for an ESOP sponsor to transfer the shares that are causing individuals to become "disqualified persons" to a plan that is not an ESOP (and hence exclude them from consideration as "deemed-owned shares"). This also seems to work where a portion of the ESOP is simply declared to be a profit sharing trust and the offending shares are moved there on the books of the plan. While one result of this process is to cure a potential "nonallocation year," it also moves the shares out of the tax shelter available only to ESOPs. If this solution comes into play, the transfer plan (profit sharing or stock bonus plan likely) will become subject to unrelated business income tax (UBIT) on its share of the earnings of the corporation. This can be a significant financial burden but is definitely preferable to the result of a nonallocation year.

Most of the fixes of this condition involve creative applications of the rules, and, since they generally discriminate against the higher-paid employees, are usually permissible under ERISA (although they may require amending your plan).

Ultimately, if you cannot create broad enough ownership through any of the legal means to do so, you may have to live as a C corporation (which, by the way, is not the end of the world—after all, all ESOPs were in C corporations up to a very few years ago).

Conclusion

Administering an S corporation ESOP certainly raises many issues. It is very unlikely, though, that the negative impact of any of these issues would outweigh the benefits of making an S corporation election for a substantially ESOP-owned company. And they can be accommodated if they are on the early agenda of any ESOP company considering the election.

CHAPTER SIX

Complying with the Section 409(p) Anti-Abuse Rules

Carolyn F. Zimmerman
Revised by Barbara M. Clough and Thomas Roback, Jr.

S hortly after the law changed to legitimize S corporation ESOPs, it became evident that the S corporation setup was vulnerable to tax avoidance schemes of such magnitude as to render the S corporation ESOP more of a tax shelter than a qualified retirement plan. With the passage of the Economic Growth and Tax Relief Reconciliation Act of 2001 (EGTRRA), the Internal Revenue Service (IRS) moved to block those schemes. The IRS holds that the intention of any ESOP must be to spread the beneficial ownership of company stock throughout the company's employee base in a fair manner as prescribed by the Employee Retirement Income Security Act of 1974 (ERISA), *not* to benefit highly compensated and major shareholders in a disproportionate manner. To this end, as part of EGTRRA, Congress enacted Section 409(p) of the Internal Revenue Code (the "Code"),[1] which sets forth a special test that must be applied to S corporation ESOPs for them to demonstrate they are not tax shelters. Final Section 409(p) regulations are effective December 20, 2006, for plan years beginning on or after January 1, 2006.

The 409(p) anti-abuse test is quite complicated. The test requires an ESOP with S corporation stock to prove that no portion of the plan assets (or assets attributable to the plan) is accrued directly or indirectly for the benefit of a "disqualified person." The test is intended to catch abusive ESOPs, but in reality it can catch almost any S corporation

---

1. Unless otherwise stated, all references to section numbers in this chapter are to the Code.

ESOP. It is very important to apply the test annually and whenever there is a change in ownership, family, leverage, or synthetic equity programs, because a plan can fail on any day of the year. The penalties are draconian and could actually cost you your company.

History

The new law was effective immediately for S corporations that adopted ESOPs after March 14, 2001, as well as for C corporations with existing ESOPs that elected S status after that date. For S corporations with ESOPs already in existence on March 14, 2001, the law takes effect for plan years beginning after December 31, 2004. Revenue Ruling 2003-6 clarifies which S corporation ESOPs are eligible to be "grandfathered" so as to have an effective date of plan years beginning after December 31, 2004.[2] Revenue Ruling 2004-4 addresses S corporation ESOPs set up within corporate structures that would not substantially benefit a broad base of company employees.[3]

The test described in Code Section 409(p) looks for:

1. Individual persons who own—or *could* own—more than 10% of specifically defined shares of the S corporation (see "deemed-owned shares" below), including ESOP stock.

2. Family groups, who own—or *could* own—20% or more of those shares of the S corporation. Once these people are identified and the stock of family members, including stock owned outright, has been attributed, if all their stock adds up to 50% or more of the outstanding shares of the company, the S corporation ESOP is deemed to be abusive and has incurred, or will incur, a "nonallocation year" together with the applicable penalties.

---

2. Rev. Ruling 2003-6 addresses S corporation ESOPs that were hastily set up before the March 14, 2001, deadline and did not substantially benefit a broad base of employees within the S corporation. These "shells" were being offered for sale as "pre-grandfathered."

3. Rev. Ruling 2004-4 sets forth three examples of corporate structures that, according to the IRS, were not only abusive S corporation ESOPs but also "listed transactions" under Code Section 6111 (tax shelters).

On July 21, 2003, the IRS issued Temporary Treasury Regulations Section 1.409(p)-1T, temporary and proposed regulations that actually strengthened the severity of the test by expanding the definition of "synthetic equity" (see below). These regulations are effective for plan years ending after October 20, 2003, for S corporation ESOPs that were not in existence on March 14, 2001.

Effective Date

On December 17, 2004, temporary regulations were published, applicable to plan years beginning on or after January 1, 2005.[4] However, the previous rules dealing with ownership structures that constitute an avoidance or evasion of Section 409(p), including the rules relating to structures similar to those addressed in Rev. Rul. 2004-4, apply for plan years ending on or after December 31, 2004.

There are three special "transition rules" included in these regulations:

1. ESOP shares that are held for a disqualified person before the first plan year beginning on or after January 1, 2005, will not be treated as an impermissible accrual in 2005 if the shares are disposed of before July 1, 2005 (e.g., by distribution or transfer to a non-ESOP), and no amount is contributed for the benefit of the disqualified person under any plan of the employer intended to meet the requirements of Section 401(a), including the ESOP, during the period from the first day of the first plan year beginning on or after January 1, 2005, through June 30, 2005. However, even if no amount is allocated to a disqualified person during this period, but this period is part of the first nonallocation year of the ESOP, an excise tax will apply under Code Section 4979A with respect to either ESOP shares held for a disqualified person or synthetic equity that is treated as owned under these regulations on the first

---

4. "Prohibited Allocations of Securities in an S Corporation," TD 9164 and REG-129709-03 (Temp. Treas. Reg. § 1.409(p)-1T), 69 Fed. Reg. 75455 (Dec. 17, 2004), corrected in 70 Fed. Reg. 11121 (March 8, 2005) (removing Section 1.409(p)–1T(d)(2)(iv)).

day of the plan year, regardless of whether there is an impermissible accrual or impermissible allocation.

2. The 2004 person-by-person rules regarding how to determine whether a person is a disqualified person and whether a year is a nonallocation year generally do not go into effect until July 1, 2005. However, a rule excludes from the formula for determining a "disqualified person" synthetic equity that is not likely ever to be exercised (e.g., having an exercise price that is more than 200% of the fair market value of the shares on the date of grant), if that synthetic equity were to prevent a nonallocation year from occurring.

3. The 2004 rules, including those relating to the right to receive shares with disproportional voting rights (see "Synthetic Equity," below), did not go into effect until July 1, 2005, so long as there would be no prohibited allocation before then under these regulations if the 2004 rules relating to the right to receive shares with disproportional voting rights were disregarded.

The final 409(p) regulations became effective on December 20, 2006, and are applicable for plan years beginning on or after January 1, 2006. The final regulations included a number of significant differences and clarifications from the 2004 temporary regulations, such as:

- Definitions
- Reshuffling
- Treatment of deemed distributions
- Prevention measures
- Right of first refusal clarification
- Acceleration of triennial determination date
- Violation consequences

The definition of "employer" was added to the final regulations and references Treasury Regulations Section 1.410(b)-9, which defines it as the employer sponsoring the plan and all employers that are members of the controlled group of the plan sponsor. The final regulations also refined the definition of "family member" as a disqualified person only if he or she also owns deemed-owned ESOP shares or synthetic equity. Also, the provision in the previous regulations requiring attribution of ownership under Section 318 was deleted from the final regulations. The final regulations also clarified that, in determining the present value of nonqualified deferred compensation, a "reasonable" discount rate should be used.

The 2006 regulations also indicate that reshuffling, a previous correction method for a 409(p) problem, will most likely violate the nondiscriminatory requirements of Section 401(a)(4). Both the IRS and the Treasury Department support this interpretation. Nonetheless, the final regulations do not actually prohibit reshuffling.

The final regulations also added an amendment to Section 402 covering eligible rollover distributions. This amendment added deemed distributions pursuant to 409(p) to the list of payments that are not eligible rollovers. This addition extends to the proposed Roth regulations. Therefore, a deemed distribution is also not a qualified distribution from a Roth 401(k) account.

The preamble to the final regulations listed several noteworthy 409(p) prevention methods. The only preventive measure that is guaranteed to also pass muster under Section 401(a)(4) is a transfer to a non-ESOP account. More detailed requirements to facilitate this kind of transfer were also detailed, such as consistent benefit statements after the transfer, and an affirmative action taken no later than the date of the transfer (retroactive transfers are prohibited). Note that the unrelated business income tax (UBIT) will apply for this kind of transfer. Other methods are listed such as: reducing contributions for HCEs (highly compensated employees) who may become disqualified persons, expanding ESOP coverage to include all employees, providing additional benefits to NHCEs (non-highly compensated employees), or mandatory diversification of stock in the accounts of HCEs who are qualified participants under the statutory diversification provisions.

The final regulations also clarified that an individual first right of refusal to buy ESOP shares is not considered synthetic equity as long as two conditions are met:

1. The first right of refusal would not be taken into account in determining whether the S corporation has a second class of stock, and

2. The price to acquire stock under the first right of refusal is not less than the price paid to buy stock from participants pursuant to the Section 409(h) put right.

These final regulations retain the previous rules regarding calculating of the number of shares of synthetic equity that are not determined by reference to shares of stock of the S corporation. In addition, the new rules still permit the number of synthetic equity shares treated as owned on a determination date to remain constant for up to a three-year period from that date (the triennial method). However, the new rules include changes in the triennial methodology to permit the ability, during the three-year period, to accelerate a determination date prospectively in the event of a change in the plan year or any merger, consolidation, or transfer of ESOP assets under Section 414(l).

The final regulations retain the previous consequences of 409(p) failure that the ESOP fails to satisfy the requirements of Section 4975(e)(7) and is no longer considered to be an ESOP. The final regulations expand the consequences of a failure to include termination of the entity's S corporation election and disqualification of the ESOP due to operational noncompliance. The new rules also clarify that a 409(p) violation does not provide an exemption from prohibited transaction rules for exempt loans.

Definitions

In describing the 409(p) test, this chapter uses the following terms, defined specifically for our purposes:

Disqualified Person

A disqualified person is described according to the following rules:

1. *10% Individual Rule:* Anyone who holds 10% or more of the deemed-owned shares, including synthetic equity if applicable.
2. *20% Family Rule:* Anyone *and* his or her family members who together hold 20% or more of the deemed-owned shares, including synthetic equity if applicable.

3. *Special Family Member Rule:* Anyone not already described in (1) or (2) above who holds any amount of deemed-owned shares and is a family member of a disqualified person under the 20% family rule. "Member of the family" means, with respect to an individual:

    a. the spouse of the individual

    b. an ancestor or lineal descendant of the individual or individual's spouse

    c. a brother or sister of the of the individual or individual's spouse, and any lineal descendant of the brother or sister

    d. a spouse of any individual described in b or c above

The spouse of an individual who is legally separated under a decree of divorce or separate maintenance is not treated as such individual's spouse. Under Code Section 409(p), the meaning of "family member" is extremely broad and may include stepsiblings or cousins.

Deemed-Owned Shares

Deemed-owned shares include shares allocated to a participant's ESOP account balance, plus shares that will be released to that account balance from a suspense account as payments are made on an exempt loan (see "Mock Allocation" below). They also include shares on which "synthetic equity" is based if inclusion will result in the individual's becoming a disqualified person. Shares owned outright are not considered to be deemed-owned shares (but will count for purposes of determining a nonallocation year—see below).

Mock Allocation

To determine the deemed-owned shares that will come from the suspense account in the future, a mock allocation is performed, using the percentage of shares to total shares as they were allocated in the most recent plan year.[5]

---

5. Although Code Section 409(p) clearly states that "mock allocation" can be calculated based on the most recent share release calculation, there is specu-

Prohibited Allocation

A prohibited allocation is either an *impermissible accrual* or an *impermissible allocation* made for the benefit of a disqualified person during a nonallocation year. An impermissible accrual occurs to the extent that stock of the sponsoring S corporation owned by the ESOP and any assets attributable thereto are held in the ESOP trust for the benefit of a disqualified person during a nonallocation year. "Assets" includes not only S corporation stock but also any distributions made on such stock, including earnings thereon, plus proceeds from the sale of S corporation securities held for the disqualified person in the ESOP (including earnings). The final regulations retained this provision despite concerns voiced by some members of the S corporation ESOP community.

An impermissible allocation is one that occurs directly or indirectly under any qualified plan of the employer to the extent the disqualified person accrues additional benefits under the ESOP or other qualified plan of the employer that, but for the nonallocation year, would otherwise have been added to his/her account and invested in employer securities consisting of stock in an S corporation owned by the ESOP.[6]

Synthetic Equity

Synthetic equity includes the underlying shares of any stock acquisition program, such as stock appreciation rights (SARs), incentive or other stock options, a similar right to future cash payments based on the stock value or appreciation in value, a right to acquire stock or assets of a related entity, nonqualified deferred compensation plans, phantom stock, warrants, restricted stock, a deferred issuance stock right, split-dollar life insurance, or any right the value of which is based on the value of underlying shares of company stock. Also included are all nonqualified deferred compensation programs, i.e., any right to receive compensation for services performed for the S corporation (or related

---

lation in the S corporation community that the prior year's ending balances could be used.

6. For a full discussion of "impermissible allocation" and "impermissible accrual," see Treas. Reg. § 1.409(p)-1T at *Federal Register*, vol. 71, no. 244, pp. 76134-45.

entities) that is deferred beyond 2½ months after the year in which services are performed.

The 2004 regulations expand the definition of synthetic equity to include the right to acquire stock or assets of a related entity. They also exclude nonqualified deferred compensation that was taken into account before January 1, 2005, for purposes of FICA (the Federal Insurance Contributions Act) and was outstanding before the first date on which the ESOP acquired any employer securities.

The 2004 regulations define synthetic equity as follows:

1. If a synthetic equity right includes a right to purchase or receive shares of S corporation stock that have per-share voting rights greater than the per-share voting rights of one or more shares of S corporation stock held by the ESOP, then the number of shares of deemed-owned synthetic equity attributable to such right is at least equal to the number of shares that would have the same voting rights if such shares had the same per-share voting rights as shares held by the ESOP.

2. The number of synthetic equity shares for nonqualified deferred compensation may be determined as of the first day of the ESOP's plan year, or any other reasonable determination date or dates during a plan year that is consistently used by the ESOP for this purpose for all persons. The date used must be reasonably representative of the share value of the S corporation's stock. The number of shares of synthetic equity treated as owned for any period from a determination date through the date immediately preceding the next following determination date is the number of shares treated as owned on the first day of that period.[7]

---

7. The ESOP may provide, on a reasonable and consistent basis used by the ESOP for this purpose for all persons, that the number of shares of synthetic equity treated as owned on an identified determination date remain constant for the period from that determination date until the date that immediately precedes the third anniversary of the identified determination date. As new grants are made during this three-year period, the appropriate number of shares of synthetic equity resulting from the new grant would be determined at the next determination date, which would likewise remain constant during the remainder or the same three-year period. The ESOP must recalculate the number of shares of this type of synthetic equity at least every three years,

3. The third rule applies to cases in which the ESOP does not own 100% of the S corporation stock. If such is the case, the number of synthetic shares otherwise determined is reduced ratably to the extent that shares of the S corporation are owned by a person who is not an ESOP (and subject to federal income taxes).[8]

Family Member

For the family aggregation tests, family members of an individual include the following:

1. The individual's spouse
2. An ancestor or lineal descendant of the individual or the individual's spouse
3. A brother or sister of the individual, or of the individual's spouse, *and* any lineal descendant of the brother or sister
4. The spouse of anyone in (2) or (3), such as in-laws, nieces, nephews, niece and nephew spouses, etc.

Note: The definition of "spouse" does not include those who are legally separated or divorced.

Triennial Recalculations

The test under Section 409(p) must be performed no less frequently than annually; however, if the terms of the ESOP so provide, synthetic equity may be redetermined not less frequently than every three years. Accordingly, a plan document may "fix" the number of shares of syn-

---

based on the S corporation share value on the applicable determination date and the aggregate present value of nonqualified deferred compensation on that determination date.

8. For example, if an S corporation has 200 outstanding shares, of which Bob owns 50 shares and the ESOP owns the other 150 shares, and Susie would be treated as owning 200 synthetic equity shares if the ESOP owned 100% of the S corporation shares, the number of synthetic shares treated as owned by Susie is decreased from 200 to 150 (because the ESOP owns only 75% of the outstanding stock of the C corporation rather than 100%).

thetic equity for a specified period beginning on the determination date and ending not later than the third anniversary of the identified determination date. It should be noted that additional accruals, allocations, or grants of synthetic equity that are made during the triennial period must be taken into account on each determination date within the period. Once a triennial determination date is set, it can be changed only through a plan amendment and must be earlier than the original triennial determination date; i.e., the date cannot be extended.

Nonallocation Year

A nonallocation year is any plan year in which disqualified persons own (or are deemed to own) at least 50% of the stock of the S corporation or at least 50% of the outstanding shares of stock in the S corporation (including deemed-owned shares).

The Test

To perform the test, you will need the following information:

- ESOP participants and shares owned, both inside and outside the ESOP
- Family relationships of ESOP participants, including persons not in the ESOP
- Owners of synthetic equity, if any

The test itself consists of two parts. In Part One, the tester looks for ESOP participants who meet the criteria for disqualified persons. If there are none, there is no need to proceed any further. However, if there is even one disqualified person, the tester must proceed to Part Two to test for a nonallocation year.

Part One

In practice, Part One consists of three steps that should be performed for every person who could be a disqualified person under Section

409(p). Theoretically, this is any person who does *not* fall into the following category:

- An ESOP participant who does not now and never will own more than 10% of the ESOP shares, both allocated and unallocated, *and*
- Does not own any synthetic equity, *and*
- Is not a family member of anyone who owns shares inside or outside the ESOP, or any form of synthetic equity.

To begin Part One, the tester may set up a spreadsheet (see the appendix to this chapter) containing all ESOP participants and owners of synthetic equity, showing the following:

- ESOP allocated stock
- ESOP "mock allocation" (participant's portion of the unallocated stock)
- Synthetic equity holdings of everyone, together with a translation into the number of shares represented (in the case of a less-than-100% ESOP, in proportion to the ESOP's ownership percentage). Synthetic equity not based on stock is converted to a number of shares equal to the present value of the synthetic equity divided by the fair market value of the S corporation stock.
- Total deemed-owned shares belonging to each participant
- Percentage of total deemed-owned shares owned by individual
- Family relationships

Using this information, you can now determine which, if any, of these people are disqualified persons.

- Step 1: Apply the 10% Individual Rule, with and without synthetic equity.
- Step 2: Apply the 20% Family Rule, with and without synthetic equity.
- Step 3: Apply the Special Family Rule.

Note: The 2004 regulations provide that, in computing the percentages, the amount of synthetic equity shares added to the denominator of the fraction consists of only those shares owned by the person, or by the person and his or her family members.

According to the regulations, the following definition applies for determining a disqualified person:[9]

> *General rule.* A disqualified person is any person for whom—
>
> (i) The number of such person's deemed-owned ESOP shares of the S corporation is at least 10 percent of the number of deemed-owned ESOP shares of the S corporation;
>
> (ii) The aggregate number of such person's deemed-owned ESOP shares and synthetic equity shares of the S corporation is at least 10 percent of the sum of:
>
> (A) The total number of deemed-owned ESOP shares, and
>
> (B) The person's synthetic equity shares of the S corporation.
>
> (iii) The aggregate number of deemed-owned ESOP shares of such person and of the members of such person's family is at least 20 percent of the number of deemed-owned ESOP shares of the S corporation; or
>
> (iv) The aggregate number of the S corporation's deemed-owned ESOP shares and synthetic equity shares of such person and of the members of such person's family is at least 20 percent of the sum of:
>
> (A) The total number of deemed-owned ESOP shares, and
>
> (B) The synthetic equity shares of the S corporation owned by such person and the members of such person's family.

Part Two

After determining which persons are disqualified persons under the rule, calculate the aggregate ownership of all disqualified persons. Include shares owned outright and apply family attribution rules. If the total number of shares owned by disqualified persons is 50% or more of the outstanding shares of the S corporation, a nonallocation year can, or has, occurred. The temporary regulations describe a "nonallocation year" as follows:[10]

> (1) *Definition generally.* A nonallocation year means a plan year of an ESOP during which, at any time, the ESOP holds any employer securities that are shares of an S corporation and either—

---

9.   Temp. Treas. Reg. § 1.409(p)-1T(d).

10.   Temp. Treas. Reg. § 1.409(p)-1T(c).

(i) Disqualified persons own at least 50 percent of the number of outstanding shares of stock in the S corporation (including deemed-owned ESOP shares), or

(ii) Disqualified persons own at least 50 percent of the sum of:

(A) The outstanding shares of stock in the S corporation (including deemed-owned ESOP shares), plus

(B) The shares of synthetic equity in the S corporation owned by disqualified persons.

Penalties

There are two tiers of punishment waiting for an S corporation ESOP that has incurred a nonallocation year.

First, the ESOP must treat as distributable (and therefore taxable) any allocation made to the account of a disqualified person in that year.

Second, the S corporation must pay an excise tax consisting of 50% of the total amount of the funds involved, including any prohibited allocations or accruals made to disqualified persons in that year as well as the total value of synthetic equity owned by disqualified persons during that year, even if they did not receive an allocation during the year.

In the first nonallocation year of an S corporation ESOP, the tax is 50% of the total value of deemed-owned shares and synthetic equity owned by all disqualified persons, even though no prohibited allocations were made during such year.

In addition, if a prohibited allocation occurs, the plan has then failed to satisfy the requirements of Section 4975(e)(7) and ceases to be an ESOP. Should this occur, the exemption from excise tax on prohibited transactions for loans to leveraged ESOPs would cease to apply, and the employer would then owe an excise tax with respect to the outstanding securities acquisition loan(s). In addition, the plan would then be considered to have not been operated in accordance with its terms and Section 409(p) and would fail to meet the plan qualification requirements, which would then cause the corporation's S election to terminate.

Avoiding a Nonallocation Year

The safest way to avoid a nonallocation year is to perform the Section 409(p) tests well in advance of the year in question. For most companies, this will mean finding a third-party administrator who is knowledgeable enough to run the test correctly. For others, they may attempt to run the tests themselves. In any case, some person at the company should be conversant with the tests even if a third-party administrator is running them.

The correction will depend upon why the company failed Section 409(p), and by how much. The reasons for failure could have to do with existing S corporation ESOP allocations, future S corporation ESOP allocations (mock allocations or future contributions), synthetic equity, or ownership of stock outside the S corporation ESOP. Remember that a correction cannot be made to the holdings of non-disqualified persons to bring the percentage of stock owned by the disqualified persons into the passing range. Any steps taken to prevent a nonallocation year must be in accordance with the terms of the plan document as well as the nondiscrimination requirements of Code Section 401(a)(4).

Corrections

Following is a list of solutions that may be used in avoiding a nonallocation year. When considering a correction, it is extremely important to fit the solution to your particular company.

- *Amend your plan to include "fail-safe" language that would allow the plan to correct the cause of a nonallocation year in any given year.* This is not a correction in itself, but it is thought to add credibility to an S corporation ESOP plan document.

- *Amend your plan to provide more liberal eligibility and allocation requirements.* This is not a correction in itself, but it if there are more eligible participants, it will dilute the stock allocation and thereby reduce the ownership percentages.

- *Elect C corporation status.* This is the ultimate correction, which may in the end be the best one depending upon your goals for equity compensation incentives inside your company and your company's particular tax situation. Smaller companies may find that the taxes they would pay as a C corporation are considerably less than the amounts of the S corporation ESOP penalties under Code Section 401(p).

- *Pay the excise tax.* Remember that the tax must be paid in every year that has incurred a nonallocation year. This is a very expensive option, but might be worth it and should be considered.

- *Amend the plan's allocation provisions to restrict participants as needed to avoid a nonallocation year.* Some S corporation ESOPs restrict plan participants from accumulating more than 10% of the total ESOP allocations and any family group from reaching the 20% level. This may be only a partial solution, depending upon family groups within the company.

- *Amend the plan to allow for in-service distributions to eliminate holdings of stock that have created disqualified persons.* This solution depends on the willingness of the plan participants to take in-service distributions. They cannot be forced into taking them. Also remember that such a provision must be nondiscriminatory. The sale must occur before a nonallocation year occurs. Analysis should occur before the sale to ensure that the sale does not result in new disqualified persons.

- *Begin profit sharing accounting ("reshuffling") to keep ESOP account balances in line with each other.* You could still have a problem if your plan is very small and 100% owned by the ESOP. However, Section 409(p) states that the test could fail if at any time during the plan year, so potentially a plan could be failing 409(p) before the "reshuffling" is performed. The final regulations indicate that absent a special rule for applying the nondiscrimination requirements of Section 401(a)(4), it could be difficult to reshuffle without violating the section.

- *Transfer the S corporation securities out of the ESOP component of the plan or to another qualified plan that is not an ESOP.* Provided the plan document allows for such a transfer, all nondiscrimination requirements under Section 401(a)(4) are considered to have been passed. The transfer must be accomplished by an affirmative action taken no later than the date of the transfer, and all subsequent actions (such as participant statements) must confirm that the transfer occurred on the set date.

- *Minimize or eliminate synthetic equity programs.* Some companies have successfully replaced these programs with cash bonus plans or other plans not tied to company stock or stock performance. Remember that, according to the temporary regulations, even nonqualified deferred compensation plans are considered to be synthetic equity if not paid within 2½ months after the close of the year in which services are performed.

- *Have the company redeem and retire or recontribute ESOP shares.* This helps keep shares in the ESOP to a manageable percentage and allocates them across a broad range of participants.

- *Match 401(k) deferrals with company stock.* This increases the base of ownership within the ESOP.

- *Lower individual direct ownership levels through a sale to the ESOP or another buyer.* Consider family relationships.

The most important thing for S corporation ESOP sponsors to take into account is that the IRS is very serious about disallowing S corporation ESOPs that may not be broad-based under the definitions and requirements of Code Section 409(p). Consider what Section 409(p)(7) says:

> (A) *In general.* The Secretary shall prescribe such regulations as may be necessary to carry out the purposes of this subsection.
>
> (B) *Avoidance or evasion.* The Secretary may, by regulation or other guidance of general applicability, provide that a nonallocation year occurs in any case in which the principal purpose of the ownership structure of an S corporation constitutes an avoidance or evasion of this subsection.

Thus, the Secretary has the broadest powers to interpret Section 409(p) and can issue rulings as seen fit to prevent abuses. Revenue Rulings 2003-6 and 2004-4 are examples of cases in which IRS moved both appropriately and quickly to prevent abusive situations.

S corporation ESOPs must take every precaution to prevent a nonallocation year. S corporation ESOP sponsors have no choice but to take the matter seriously. To end with another quote from the temporary regulations:[11]

> (3) *Special rule for avoidance or evasion.*
>   . . . .

---

11. Temp. Treas. Reg. § 1.409(p)-1T (c)(3).

(ii) Under section 409(p)(7)(B), the Commissioner, in revenue rulings, notices, and other guidance published in the Internal Revenue Bulletin (see §601.601(d)(2)(ii)(*b*) of this chapter), may provide that a nonallocation year occurs in any case in which the principal purpose of the ownership structure of an S corporation constitutes an avoidance or evasion of section 409(p). *For any year that is a nonallocation year under this paragraph (c)(3), the Commissioner may treat any person as a disqualified person* [Emphasis added].

Sources

Following are some useful materials that contain analyses and examples of Section 409(p) testing.

Ackerman, David. "Legal Considerations for S Corporation ESOPs." Chapter 2 of this book.

Grussing, Bruce D., and Susan D. Lenczewski. "The Tax Free Environment of S Corporations and the Perils of the Anti-Abuse Rules." *Business Entities* 6, no. 2 (March/April 2004).

"Legal Update." *The ESOP Report* (The ESOP Association), September 2003.

Rosen, Corey. "IRS Cracks Down on ESOP S Corporation Deferred Compensation Scams." Web page at the site of the National Center for Employee Ownership, www.nceo.org.

Internal Revenue Service and Treasury. "Prohibited Allocations of Securities in an S Corporation" [final regulations]. *Federal Register*, December 20, 2006 (vol. 71, no. 244).

Appendix 6-A. Sample 409(p) Anti-Abuse Test

Disqualified Persons Determination

NAME	ALLOCATED ESOP SHARES	MOCK STOCK	SYNTHETIC EQUITY	TOTAL DEEMED -OWNED SHARES	INDIVIDUAL % W/SYNTHETIC EQUITY	INDIVIDUAL % W/NO SYNTHETIC EQUITY
Jack	100.00	15.00	5.50	120.50	10.31%	9.89%
Ursula	40.00	9.00	6.50	55.50	4.75%	4.21%
Gail	50.00	21.00	0.00	71.00	6.10%	6.10%
Sandy	30.00	4.00	0.00	34.00	2.92%	2.92%
Jennifer	13.00	6.00	0.00	19.00	1.63%	1.63%
Others	600.00	275.00	0.00	875.00	75.24%	75.24%
	833.00	330.00	12.00	1,175.00		

Calculate Family Percentage

NAME	ALLOCATED ESOP SHARES	MOCK STOCK	SYNTHETIC EQUITY	TOTAL DEEMED -OWNED SHARES	INDIVIDUAL % W/SYNTHETIC EQUITY	INDIVIDUAL % W/NO SYNTHETIC EQUITY
Jack	100.00	15.00	5.50	120.50	10.31%	9.89%
Ursula	40.00	9.00	6.50	55.50	4.75%	4.21%
Gail	50.00	21.00	0.00	71.00	6.10%	6.10%
Sandy	30.00	4.00	0.00	34.00	2.92%	2.92%
					24.08%	23.12%

Run 409(p) Test

DISQUALIFIED PERSONS	ESOP SHARES	MOCK STOCK SHARES	SYNTHETIC EQUITY	OUTRIGHT SHARES	TOTAL OWNERSHIP
Jack	100.00	15.00	5.50	200.00	320.50
Ursula	40.00	9.00	6.50	5.00	60.50
Gail	50.00	21.00	0.00	6.00	77.00
Sandy	30.00	4.00	0.00	0.00	34.00
Subtotal	220.00	49.00	12.00	211.00	492.00
Others	613.00	281.00	0.00	0.00	1,386.00

Calculation: 26.20%

NONALLOCATION YEAR?   **NO**

CHAPTER SEVEN

Phantom Stock and SARs in S Corporation ESOP Companies

Corey Rosen

One of the most common calls we get at the National Center for Employee Ownership (NCEO) is from S corporations that want certain key employees to participate in the equity growth of the company but who do not want employees to actually end up with shares. In 100% S corporation ESOP companies, having employees end up being owners of shares means that distributions would have to be paid both to them and, in much larger numbers, to the ESOP. With less-than-100% ESOPs, this may also be a concern, but there is also considerable uncertainty about whether stock options, the more traditional way of sharing ownership with key people, creates a second class of stock. S corporations can only have one class of stock.

Phantom stock and stock appreciation rights (SARs) can address these issues. Based on NCEO survey data, about 20% of S corporation ESOP companies provide some kind of individual equity to people outside the ESOP. Appealing as these approaches can be, S corporation ESOP companies must be cautious in how they are used. First, ESOP fiduciaries should not allow the board to award grants beyond what would be considered reasonable based on what these individuals might be able to earn on the market or, alternatively, how much added value they bring to the company. Second, phantom stock and stock appreciation rights count as "synthetic equity" and, as such, are subject to the anti-abuse rules described elsewhere in this book.

Phantom Stock and SARs Defined

SARs and phantom stock are very similar concepts. Both are bonus plans that grant not stock but rather the right to receive an award based on the value of the company's stock, hence the terms "appreciation rights" and "phantom." The awards can pay out in cash or stock, but normally would pay out only in cash in S corporation ESOP companies.

A SAR is like a stock option without the stock: it generally can be exercised freely at a point after vesting (or upon the occurrence of a specified event) and before the end of its term. At exercise, the company pays the SAR plan participant the amount that the share price has appreciated between the grant date and the exercise date, multiplied by the number of shares specified in the grant.

In contrast, with phantom stock the plan participant receives a "phantom" grant of hypothetical shares that provides him or her with the full value of the shares at a given date or upon the occurrence of a specified event. Phantom stock plans often credit the accounts of participants with dividends, in which case the ultimate payout reflects what a holder of actual shares would have received if such events occurred. If there are stock splits, phantom stock or SARs would normally be adjusted to reflect that change.

The form of SAR and phantom stock plans is not defined by law. As described below, they are flexible and can have a variety of features. However, the Section 409A deferred compensation rules impose certain restrictions that affect design decisions.

Eligibility: Companies can provide phantom stock or SARs to anyone—employees, board members, contractors, or anyone else. If a company makes these awards broadly available to employees, however, there is a chance they could be considered "qualified employee benefit plans" falling under the same legal umbrella as retirement plans governed by ERISA (the Employee Retirement Income Security Act of 1974, as amended), especially if they are designed to pay out only at or after termination of employment. If so, they would have to meet a variety of ERISA-based rules for testing plan operations to make sure they do not discriminate in favor of more highly compensated employees. If the plans are designed so that the awards are paid out periodically, such as every three to five years when a particular tranche of awards vests, they would not be considered retirement plans. Many phantom stock and SAR plans are designed to pay out in this way, as opposed to at termination, retirement, or sale of the company, and so should not run afoul of these rules.

Plans that do restrict payout until termination, retirement, or sale of the company will avoid ERISA coverage if they fall into the exemption for a "top-hat plan," which is an unfunded[1] deferred compensation plan maintained primarily for "a select group of management or highly compensated employees." Many practitioners believe that a good rule of thumb is that if 15% or fewer of all employees are eligible, the plan will qualify for the top-hat exemption. Of course, most ESOP companies using phantom and SAR plans are providing the awards only to a very limited number of people.

Vesting: Vesting can be based on whatever criteria the employer chooses. Most plans use time-based vesting, typically not more than five years. Vesting may be "cliff" (all at once) or graduated. Many plans, however, are performance-vested, meaning they vest only when a certain individual, group, or corporate target is met. Phantom plans that condition the receipt of the award on meeting certain financial or other performance objectives are sometimes also called "performance unit plans." A few plans provide vesting only on termination or sale of the company. Companies can also use "double triggers," meaning vesting occurs only when two requirements have been met, most typically both service and performance requirements.

Settlement Dates: Once the awards are fully vested, phantom stock usually has a specific settlement date when the award is paid out, whereas employees can typically choose when to exercise their vested SARs. Phantom stock and SARs, like nonstatutory stock options, result in income taxes when the employee receives the payout. Plan designers have flexibility to set payout dates or events but should be mindful of the deferred compensation tax rules associated with Code Section 409A. For SARs that are not designed to be exempt from deferred com-

---

1. In this context, "unfunded" means only that the employer has not irrevocably set aside assets to fund the plan, putting such assets beyond the reach of general creditors.

pensation rules and for phantom stock, that means an employer that wants to allow deferral beyond vesting should adhere to the rules on the timing of deferral elections discussed in the deferred compensation section of this chapter.

Settlement Form: SARs and phantom stock can be settled in cash or in shares. Settling in shares might be appropriate in less than 100% ESOPs. SARs that pay out in stock have more favorable accounting treatment than SARs that pay out in cash, as discussed briefly in the section on accounting in this chapter. Phantom stock awards settled in shares are essentially the same concept as "restricted stock units (RSUs)." The common parlance is to refer to phantom stock when discussing awards paid out in cash, but RSUs when discussing those that pay out in shares. These are terms of art, however, not terms of law. In fact, some companies refer to phantom stock as "shadow" stock or some other term, often because they see "phantom" stock as almost pejorative.

Dividends, Voting Rights, and Other Shareholder Rights: Phantom stock may pay a kind of phantom dividend, a payment equal to the dividends an owner of that actual number of shares would receive. Because this is not an actual dividend, it would be taxed as ordinary income, It is possible, however, this practice could raise "second class of stock" issues for S corporations and would make the valuation of the phantom awards more complicated. We at the NCEO do not know of S corporation ESOP companies that pay dividends on phantom stock. SARs could in theory pay dividend equivalents as well, although this is a less common design feature (the dividends would be based on the underlying number of shares, and thus not specifically linked to the increase in share value). The payment must be separate from the payout of the award itself to avoid deferred compensation tax treatment.[2] When the payout is made, it is taxed as ordinary income to the employee and is deductible by the employer. Neither phantom stock nor SARs carry voting rights or other shareholder control rights.

---

2. The IRS considers direct dividends on unvested SARs and stock options to be tantamount to offering a discount on the exercise price. Under Code Section 409A, the recipients of discounted stock options and SARs are subject to steep taxes and penalties.

Term: A SAR that can be exercised past its vesting date will have an expiration date beyond which it is no longer exercisable; that additional period constitutes its term. For instance, an award might provide for vesting after 5 years but allow exercise for up to 10 years.

Taxation

As noted above, phantom stock and SARs are taxable as income once the employee has received the payout. That means that once an award is exercised, it is taxable to the employee. The employee pays tax on the benefit received as if it were ordinary income; the employer gets a corresponding deduction.

Deferred Compensation Rules

This tax treatment will be less favorable if the awards do not comply with Section 409A deferred compensation rules. These rules were passed in 2004 to prevent companies from using deferred compensation as a tax avoidance or reduction strategy.

Phantom stock is subject to the deferred compensation rules associated with Section 409A. SAR designers have a choice between granting SARs that are exempt from or comply with Section 409A. To be exempt, a SAR award must meet four requirements:

- The payout cannot be more than the difference between the stock's fair market value on the grant date and fair market value on the payout date, and it must be made on the date of exercise.
- The grant price must be at or above the grant date fair market value.
- The number of shares covered by the award must be known on the grant date.
- The income cannot be deferred beyond the exercise date.

The employee can choose when to exercise this kind of SAR after vesting, making it much like a stock option except that the employee does not have to pay an exercise price.

Fair market value for this purpose is defined as the price of the shares on the public market when the award is issued, or, if there is no public market, as determined by an outside appraisal firm or through another approach the IRS deems "reasonable."

If the employer does not want to abide by these rules—for example, it wants the award's exercise price to be lower than the grant date fair market value or to determine the number of shares subject to the award some time after the grant date—then it can design a SAR award to comply with Section 409A. In that case, the employer will generally specify a payout date or event instead of allowing the employee to choose when to exercise the award. The timing of such payments is also subject to the rules regarding deferred payments, which are set out in the chapter on deferred compensation.

For both SARs and phantom stock, S corporation ESOP companies should use the ESOP-determined fair market value to grant awards as the safest way to avoid regulatory scrutiny and S corporation "second class of stock" issues.

SARs subject to Section 409A may vest based on performance criteria as long as the performance period is at least one year and the compensation is based solely on appreciation of the value of the stock. The performance criteria can be determined up to 90 days after the grant. Criteria can be subjective, but the more specific they are, the less likely they are to run afoul of the rules.

The holders of awards that are neither compliant with nor exempt from the deferred compensation rules face steep taxes and penalties.

Liquidity

Because SARs and phantom stock are essentially cash bonuses, companies need to figure out how to pay for them. Even if awards are paid out in shares (as in stock-settled SARs or RSUs), employees will want to sell the shares, at least in sufficient amounts to pay their taxes. The ESOP, of course, can be a market for this stock.

If a sale of shares to the ESOP is not planned, such as when the award is paid in cash (as is typical), some form of company funding is needed. The company can just make a promise to pay out of future cash flow. If the company wants to provide more assurance to the employee, it can put cash aside as the award builds in value. This can be held in general reserves (subject to an excess accumulated earnings tax if the number becomes too large), but that would make the money available for any other business use. An alternative is to sequester the money in a "rabbi trust" (named for a ruling involving a rabbi), a deferred compensation arrangement in which funds are placed in a trust whose assets are available to creditors in the event of the company's insolvency. Because the trust's funds are subject to forfeiture in the event of insolvency, the beneficiary is not taxed until the award vests and is paid. Rules for the operation of rabbi trusts have become more specific, and such trusts should be established with the advice of qualified counsel. The company (not the employee) is taxed on any income from the trust, and the company cannot take a tax deduction for the funds until they are paid to the employee.

Accounting Issues

Phantom stock and cash-settled SARs are subject to liability accounting, meaning the accounting costs associated with them are not settled until they pay out or expire. For cash-settled SARs, the compensation expense for awards is estimated each quarter using an option-pricing model and then trued up when the SAR is settled; for phantom stock, the underlying value is calculated each quarter and trued up through the final settlement date. Phantom stock is treated in the same way as deferred cash compensation.

In contrast, if a SAR is settled in stock, then the accounting is the same as for an option. The company must record the fair value of the award at grant and recognize expense ratably over the expected service period. If the award is performance-vested, the company must estimate how long it will take to meet the goal. If the performance measurement is tied to the company's stock price, it must use an option-pricing model to determine whether and when the goal will be met.

Choosing Plans

SARs generally make the most sense for companies that anticipate meaningful share value increases; phantom stock plans are more common in companies with more stable values. Companies need to give out more units of SARs to equal smaller grants of phantom stock if they want to provide reasonably equivalent values at grant.

To understand why this is so, imagine that a company is choosing between how many units of phantom stock to give out versus how many units of SARs. An appraisal firm would tell you that for every unit of a full-value award like phantom stock, you could give out two, three, or more units of SARs, depending on the prospects for your company and how volatile the stock price is. That's because the SAR has value only if the share price goes up, but phantom stock has value even if it goes down. It is the same as the difference between giving someone a share and giving someone an option that is valuable only if share prices increase. If most of the future value rests in appreciation, then the employee who is granted SARs may be giving up very little compared with one who is granted phantom stock. But in more mature companies, where there may be less appreciation, the SAR holder would be giving up a lot.

In companies with highly volatile stock, there is the risk that how much SARs holders get will be a result of the luck of the draw. Say a company's stock goes from $3 to $15 in the first year, from $15 to $6 in the year after that, from $6 back to $20 in year three, and $20 to $14 in year four. If employee A comes when stock is at $3, and it vests three years later at $20, he is very happy. If employee B comes along the next year when it is $15 and has options that vest in three years when it drops to $14, she is very unhappy. To mitigate this, it is better to give out smaller grants more frequently than to "front-load" awards on entry.

Anti-Abuse Issues

These issues are discussed in detail in a separate chapter, so suffice it to say here that all forms of "synthetic equity" are factored into the anti-abuse calculations. The anti-abuse law was passed to prevent the value of S corporation ESOP companies from being captured by one or a small number of employees. To do that, companies perform a two-step calculation to determine (1) who owns 10% or more of the "deemed-owned shares" in the ESOP (or 20% for family members) and (1) if these persons (called "disqualified persons") together own 50% or more of the value of the equity in the company. "Deemed-owned shares" include shares allocated to individuals in the ESOP, a pro-rata share of unallocated shares in the ESOP, and any synthetic equity (options, stock appreciation rights, phantom stock, and many other forms of deferred compensation, including those paying in cash). This calculation of deemed-owned shares is done both for the 10%/20% rule and for the 50% rule, although their interaction can be very complicated when there are family members and synthetic equity (you'll need a specialist to review the details). The rules make it clear that deemed-owned shares include those owned by people not in the ESOP, even people not employed by the company. The idea here is to prevent the ESOP from apparently owning a given percentage of the company but, when diluted by all the synthetic equity included in deemed-owned shares, actually owning much less. If plan operations indicate that these rules are being violated, then these individuals' ownership of deemed-owned shares must be reduced within the limits, and no further allocations of ESOP contributions or forfeitures can occur for these individuals until they are compliant.

The tax penalties for violating these rules are extraordinary, so much so that they would put most companies out of business. Nonetheless, it is certainly possible to design plans that do not and will not raise these issues.

Fiduciary and Ownership Culture Issues

The ESOP fiduciary, in his or her role as shareholder, has a fiduciary responsibility to make sure the board is not wasting corporate assets, as arguably it would be by overcompensating executives or other key people. Fiduciaries should be satisfied that any synthetic equity awards are reasonable in terms of market and individual performance criteria. If for some reason the awards are not granted at the fair market value set for ESOP transactions, fiduciaries should have a fairness opinion from an independent appraiser saying that these terms are fair to the ESOP.

The fact that most S corporation ESOP companies do not provide additional equity rewards to key people reflects a different set of concerns. When we at the NCEO asked employers why they did not do this, the typical response was that it was "not their culture." Instead, they wanted everyone to get ownership on the same terms, even if that meant that some key people might get less than they might get elsewhere or, so some highly paid people (those making over $230,000 in 2008) might get less in ESOP allocations, on a percentage of pay basis, than those making less money (because pay over that amount is not considered when making allocations).

Concusion

Despite all the various legal, tax, and cultural issues, phantom stock or SARs can be a relatively simple way to provide additional equity to individual employees. It is imperative, however, that these plans be designed by and monitored by people with experience and expertise.

CHAPTER EIGHT

Ownership, Motivation, and Company Performance

Corey Rosen

The tax and financial planning benefits of ESOPs are very appealing, but potentially even more powerful is their ability, through ownership sharing, to transform corporations into more motivated, innovate organizations. But does this actually happen?

In 2000, Douglas Kruse and Joseph Blasi of Rutgers University analyzed all the ESOPs set up in closely held companies between 1988 and 1994 for which data were available. They then matched these companies to comparable non-ESOP companies and looked at the sales and employment data for the paired companies for three years before the formation of the ESOP and three years after. They found that when they indexed out for the performance of the competitor companies, the ESOP companies grew 2.3% to 2.4% faster after setting up their plans than would have been expected otherwise. That seemed to give strong evidence that ESOPs do make a significant and positive contribution to corporate performance.

Impressive as these findings were, however, they did not indicate what it was about employee ownership that caused the improved performance or whether just a subset of ESOP companies with particular characteristics account for the improved performance. Other research, however, suggests that it is the combination of employee ownership and employee involvement that really makes the difference.

Knowing the answer to the question of whether ownership motivates employees seems to also answer whether employee ownership alone improves corporate performance. Not so. In most companies, labor costs are under 30% to 40% of total costs. Motivation on its own, presumably, makes employees work harder. We often ask managers to estimate just how much more work they could hope to get from more motivated employees, based on an eight-hour day. Fifteen minutes is a typical response. That comes to just 3% more time. Three percent times even a high estimate of 40% for labor costs results in just a 1.2% savings, assuming everyone will be more motivated, which is, of course, far from true.

While a 1% improvement can be a lot of money, it is not what distinguishes really successful companies from mediocre ones. The star performers are those that react to their environment in creative, innovative ways, providing better value to their customers than competitors do. How is that achieved? Through processing information and acting on it intelligently. In most companies, information gathering is limited to a group of managers. The generation of ideas is similarly limited. So is decision-making. The assumption is that only these people have the talent, and perhaps motivation, to carry out these tasks.

In fact, no one has more daily contact with customers than employees, at least in most companies. No one is closer to the day-to-day process of making the product or providing the service than the employees. And employees often do have useful ideas they could share with management.

Thus, for a company to use employee ownership effectively, it needs to do more than motivate people to work harder at what, after all, may not be the most efficient or effective thing to do. Instead, it must enlist employee ideas and information to find the best ways to do the most important things. To do that, companies need to get employees involved. Managers should seek their opinions. Employee task forces, both ad hoc and permanent, should be established to solve problems. Quality circles and employee involvement teams can be set up. Individual jobs can be enhanced, and supervision can be limited. Suggestion systems can be implemented. This all may seem like common sense, and it is. It is not very common practice in most companies, however.

Data indicate that it *is* becoming common in employee ownership companies. In a 1987 General Accounting Office (GAO) report, about one-third of all ESOP firms had some degree of employee participation. By 1993, a study of Ohio firms by the Northeast Ohio Employee Ownership Center and Kent State University found that about 60% of the companies now had active employee involvement programs, such as autonomous work teams, total quality management, or similar programs. The incidence of participation roughly doubled after the initiation of an ownership plan. These participative firms, the GAO reported, showed strong improvements in productivity when they combined their ESOPs with participative management practices.

In a study by the National Center for Employee Ownership published in the September/October 1987 *Harvard Business Review*, we found that participative ESOP firms grew 8% to 11% faster with their plans than they would have without them. In both the NCEO and GAO studies, no other factors had any influence on the relationship between ownership and performance. Three other recent studies confirmed both the direction and magnitude of these findings. Only participation can translate the motivation of ownership into the reality of a fatter bottom line. Participation is not enough on its own, either, as hundreds of studies have shown. One reason is that few participation programs last more than five years in conventional companies. By contrast, over the last decade we have not found a single ESOP company that has dropped its program.

The structure of participation varies from company to company, but it basically boils down to employees forming groups to share information, generate ideas, and make recommendations. Taking these steps, and sticking with them, is essential.

At United Airlines, for instance, employee task teams were formed soon after the employees purchased the company. Over the ensuing two years, the teams took apart every aspect of the business, making recommendations for often-substantial changes. The teams were appointed to include a broad cross-section of employees, but anyone could volunteer to join one. The ideas helped generate hundreds of millions of dollars in cost savings and new revenues. Ironically, when the teams completed their work, management backed away from the idea of participation, causing the airline some well-reported difficulties in the years that followed. The ESOP is now terminated, but most managers and employees feel that it was not a failure. United shows clearly that just setting up an ESOP, and even starting off in the right direction, is not enough. Companies must commit to a long-term ownership culture.

Stone Construction Equipment Company in Honeoye, New York, is a good example. An ESOP it set up in the late 1970s was having little impact. Then the company hired a new president, Bob Fien, who started a participative management program. Eventually, all employees were trained in "just-in-time" management and organized into work cells that schedule and control their own workflow and have considerable input into the design and organization of their jobs. Stone had been limping along and had developed a reputation for poor quality; by 1991, the company had made so much progress that *Industry Week* named it one of America's top 10 manufacturers.

At SRC Holdings in Springfield, Missouri, employee owners are taught to read detailed financial and production data. Meeting in work groups, they go over the numbers then figure out ways to improve them. Employees are sometimes given 90-page financial statements to digest. SRC's stock went from 10 cents a share when it started its ESOP in 1983, to $21 in 1994, to $83 in 2003. Employment increased more than 700%.

Other approaches include forming committees that allow employees to advise management, eliminating levels of supervision while giving nonmanagement employees more authority, holding meetings between management and randomly selected groups of employees, placing suggestion boxes, and doing anything else companies can imagine to get people involved.

The benefits of "high-involvement" management have, of course, become conventional wisdom, if still unconventional practice, at many companies. Is ownership really essential to make it work? There are no conclusive data on this, but there is good reason to believe that ownership, if not essential, is at least highly desirable. First, ownership is a cumulative benefit. Each additional year, an employee has more and more at stake in how well the company performs. It is not unusual in mature plans for the appreciation in share value and employer contributions to add up to 30% to 50% or more of pay in a year. With profit sharing or gainsharing, both of which are paid periodically and almost always amount to a small portion of total compensation, the benefit always remains relatively minor. Second, ownership has a stronger emotive appeal. People may be very proud to say they are an owner; few would brag to friends they are a profit-sharer. Finally, only ownership encourages people to think about all aspects of a business, not just short-term profits or some efficiency measure. This is especially important in companies moving toward open-book management systems.

About the Authors

David Ackerman is a partner in the Chicago office of Morgan, Lewis & Bockius, LLP, a national law firm, where he is a co-chair of the ESOP practice group. Mr. Ackerman's law practice is concentrated on ESOPs. He has advised hundreds of corporations and their shareholders and directors regarding the use of ESOPs in a wide variety of transactions, including leveraged buyouts, corporate stock repurchases, ownership succession transactions, and corporate reorganizations. He also regularly serves as legal counsel to ESOP trustees and lenders. Mr. Ackerman has provided legal counseling in several of the largest and most complex ESOP transactions, most recently including the $8.6 billion Tribune Company transaction. Mr. Ackerman has lectured and written extensively on ESOPs. He received his J.D. from Harvard Law School in 1974 and his A.B. from Princeton University in 1971.

Kathryn F. Aschwald, CFA, ASA, and **Donna J. Walker**, CFA, ASA, are principals of Columbia Financial Advisors, Inc., a business appraisal and financial advisory firm headquartered in Portland, Oregon. Columbia Financial Advisors, Inc. is nationally recognized for its expertise in ESOP appraisal and financial advisory services. Ms. Aschwald is a member of the ESOP Association's Valuation Advisory Committee and is a past chair of that committee and is a member of the ESOP Association's Interdisciplinary Committee on Fiduciary Issues. She also is on the editorial board of the *Journal of Employee Ownership Law and Finance*. Ms. Walker is the course developer for the American Society of Appraiser's ESOP Valuation Course. Both Ms. Aschwald and Ms. Walker have significant experience in ESOP-related appraisal and fairness issues and are frequent speakers, lecturers, and teachers on the subject of ESOP appraisal and financial advice.

Barbara M. Clough is a senior plan administrator at Blue Ridge ESOP Associates. Barbara has over 20 years of experience in ESOP and 401(k) plan administration. Barbara was the manager of the ESOP department of a mid-size pension consultant, where she was responsible for the training and oversight of a staff of 12 administrators. Barbara's clients included C corporation and S corporation companies, both private and publicly held, with plans ranging in size from 20 to 20,000 employees. Barbara has extensive experience with ERISA law, Department of Labor regulations, Internal Revenue Code compliance, and IRS and DOL audits. She has worked closely with plan sponsors, accountants, and legal counsel to provide guidance on plan design and to resolve plan issues such as compliance matters and audit discrepancies. Barbara graduated with a BS from Southeastern Massachusetts University. She is a member of the ESOP Association and the National Center for Employee Ownership (NCEO) and has spoken at ESOP Association and NCEO conferences.

Renee Lewis is a senior associate in the law firm of Morgan, Lewis & Bockius, LLP, an international law firm with over 1,250 lawyers in 20 offices throughout the world. She is a member of the Morgan Lewis ESOP team. She counsels financial institutions, companies, and trustees in the structuring, negotiating, and documentation of ESOP transactions, including leveraged buyouts, equity repurchases, and corporate reorganizations. She also counsels lenders and borrowers in structuring, negotiating, and documenting the terms and conditions of secured transactions, and she counsels companies in structuring, negotiating, and documenting mergers and acquisitions. Ms. Lewis earned her J.D. from DePaul University College of Law in 1997, and her B.S. from De-Paul University in 1992. She acknowledges the assistance of Ms. Julie Govreau, an associate in Morgan Lewis's Chicago office, and of Mr. Daniel Carmody, an associate in Morgan Lewis's Philadelphia office, in preparing her chapter.

Anthony I. Mathews is a senior consultant at the Beyster Institute at the Rady School of Management, UC San Diego. He joined the Beyster Institute after retiring from a nearly 30-year long career as one of the best-known ESOP and employee ownership experts in the U.S. He is a founding member of the Administrative Advisory Committee of the ESOP Association (TEA) and a former director of TEA. He is also a member of the steering committee of TEA's Western States Chapter. He serves as the chair of the board of directors of the National Center for Employee Ownership and has been a member of many other associations with interests in employee ownership, pensions, and related matters. Tony also serves as an independent, outside director for several employee ownership companies in California. Tony received his BA from Loyola University of Los Angeles in 1971 and his MA from UCLA in 1976.

Thomas Roback, Jr., CEP, QKA, is a managing director at Blue Ridge ESOP Associates. Tom has worked in the accounting, investment, and ESOP industry for over 17 years. He is an expert in the design, implementation, and execution of ESOP, stock option, stock purchase, and restricted stock plans. Mr. Roback received his MBA from the University of Baltimore and a BS in Accounting from the College of William and Mary. He is a Qualified 401(k) Administrator, Certified Equity Professional, and Capital Area Regional Vice President of the ESOP Association's Mid-Atlantic Chapter. He is a member of the ESOP Association and the National Center for Employee Ownership.

Corey Rosen is the executive director and cofounder of the National Center for Employee Ownership (NCEO). He cofounded the NCEO in 1981 after working for five years as a professional staff member in the U.S. Senate, where he helped draft legislation on employee ownership plans. Before that, he taught political science at Ripon College. He is the author or coauthor of many books and over 100 articles on employee ownership, and coauthor (with John Case and Martin Staubus) of *Equity: Why Employee Ownership Is Good for Business* (Harvard Business School Press, 2005). He was the subject of an extensive interview in *Inc.* magazine in August 2000; has appeared frequently on CNN, PBS, NPR, and other network programs; and is regularly quoted in the *Wall Street Journal*, the *New York Times*, and other leading publications. He has a Ph.D. in political science from Cornell University and serves on the advisory board of the Certified Equity Professional Institute. He is also a board member of the Great Place to Work Institute, creator of *Fortune* magazine's "100 Best Companies to Work for in America" list.

Carolyn Zimmerman is a past member of the board of directors of the ESOP Association and past chair of the ESOP Association's Advisory Committee Chairs Council. Before entering the ESOP world, she spent 10 years in the financial services industry, where she began dealing with ERISA plans in 1985. She holds a BA from Duke University and an MLS from Columbia University (New York City).

About the NCEO

The National Center for Employee Ownership (NCEO) is widely considered to be the leading authority in employee ownership in the U.S. and the world. Established in 1981 as a nonprofit information and membership organization, it now has over 2,500 members, including companies, professionals, unions, government officials, academics, and interested individuals. It is funded entirely through the work it does.

The NCEO's mission is to provide the most objective, reliable information possible about employee ownership at the most affordable price possible. As part of the NCEO's commitment to providing objective information, it does not lobby or provide ongoing consulting services. The NCEO publishes a variety of materials on employee ownership and participation, holds dozens of seminars, Webinars, and conferences on employee ownership annually, and offers a variety of online courses. The NCEO's work includes extensive contacts with the media, both through articles written for trade and professional publications and through interviews with reporters. It has written or edited several books for outside publishers. The NCEO maintains an extensive Web site at www.nceo.org.

See the following page for information on membership benefits and fees. To join, see the order form at the end of this section, visit our Web site at www.nceo.org, or telephone us at 510-208-1300.

Membership Benefits

NCEO members receive the following benefits:

- The bimonthly newsletter *Employee Ownership Report*, which covers ESOPs, equity compensation, and employee participation.
- Access to the members-only area of the NCEO's Web site, which includes a searchable newsletter archive, a discussion forum, a database of service providers, and more.

- Substantial discounts on publications, online courses, and events produced by the NCEO.

- Free access to live Webinars on ESOPs and related topics.

- The right to contact the NCEO for answers to general or specific questions regarding employee ownership.

An introductory NCEO membership costs $90 for one year ($100 outside the U.S.) and covers an entire company at all locations, a single professional offering services in this field, or a single individual with a business interest in employee ownership. Full-time students and faculty members who are not employed in the business sector may join at the academic rate of $40 for one year ($50 outside the U.S.).

Selected NCEO Publications

The NCEO offers a variety of publications on all aspects of employee ownership and participation. Below are some of our publications.

We publish new books and revise old ones on a yearly basis. To obtain the most current information on what we have available, visit us on the Web at www.nceo.org or call us at 510-208-1300.

Employee Stock Ownership Plans (ESOPs)

- *The ESOP Reader* is an overview of the issues involved in establishing and operating an ESOP. It covers the basics of ESOP rules, feasibility, valuation, and other matters, and includes brief case studies.

  $25 for NCEO members, $35 for nonmembers

- *Selling to an ESOP* is a guide for owners, managers, and advisors of closely held businesses, with a particular focus on the tax-deferred Section 1042 "rollover" for C corporation owners.

  $25 for NCEO members, $35 for nonmembers

- *Leveraged ESOPs and Employee Buyouts* discusses how ESOPs borrow money to buy out entire companies, purchase shares from a retiring owner, or finance new capital.

  $25 for NCEO members, $35 for nonmembers

- *S Corporation ESOPs* introduces the reader to how ESOPs work and then discusses the legal, valuation, administrative, and other issues associated with S corporation ESOPs.

  $25 for NCEO members, $35 for nonmembers

- *The ESOP Communications Sourcebook* provides ideas for and examples of communicating an ESOP to employees and customers. It includes a CD with communications materials, including many documents that readers can customize for their own companies.

  $35 for NCEO members, $50 for nonmembers

- *ESOP Valuation* brings together and updates where needed the best articles on ESOP valuation that we have published in our *Journal of Employee Ownership Law and Finance*, described below.

  $25 for NCEO members, $35 for nonmembers

- *ESOPs and Corporate Governance* covers everything from shareholder rights to the impact of Sarbanes-Oxley to choosing a fiduciary.

  $25 for NCEO members, $35 for nonmembers

- *Executive Compensation in ESOP Companies* discusses executive compensation issues, special ESOP considerations, and the first-ever survey of executive compensation in ESOP companies.

  $25 for NCEO members, $35 for nonmembers

- *The Inside Fiduciary Handbook* provides an overview of the issues involved in being a fiduciary at an ESOP company.

  $10 for NCEO members, $15 for nonmembers

- *How ESOP Companies Handle the Repurchase Obligation* has essays and recent research on the subject.

  $25 for NCEO members, $35 for nonmembers

- *Administrative Issues for ESOP Companies* is a guide to the issues that arise in operating an ESOP, from filing Form 5500 to dealing with Internal Revenue Service or Department of Labor audits.

  $25 for NCEO members, $35 for nonmembers

- *Model ESOP* provides a sample ESOP plan, with alternative provisions given to tailor the plan to individual needs. It also includes a section-by-section explanation of the plan and other supporting materials.

    $50 for NCEO members, $75 for nonmembers

- *Executive Compensation in ESOP Companies* discusses executive compensation issues, special ESOP considerations, and the first-ever survey of executive compensation in ESOP companies.

    $25 for NCEO members, $35 for nonmembers

Equity Compensation

- *The Stock Options Book* is a straightforward, comprehensive overview covering the legal, accounting, regulatory, and design issues involved in implementing a stock option or stock purchase plan.

    $25 for NCEO members, $35 for nonmembers

- *Selected Issues in Equity Compensation* is more detailed and specialized than *The Stock Options Book*, with chapters on issues such as repricing, securities issues, and evergreen options.

    $25 for NCEO members, $35 for nonmembers

- *The Decision-Maker's Guide to Equity Compensation* describes the various types of equity compensation, how they work, and how to decide much to give and to whom. Includes a CD with an audiovisual presentation on sharing equity.

    $35 for NCEO members, $50 for nonmembers

- *Beyond Stock Options* is a complete guide, including annotated model plans, to phantom stock, restricted stock, stock appreciation rights, performance awards, and more. Includes a CD with plan documents.

    $35 for NCEO members, $50 for nonmembers

- *Accounting for Equity Compensation* is a guide to the accounting rules that govern equity compensation programs in the U.S.

    $35 for NCEO members, $50 for nonmembers

- *Equity-Based Compensation for Multinational Corporations* describes how companies can use stock options and other equity-based programs across the world. It includes a country-by-country summary of tax and legal issues as well as a detailed case study.

  $25 for NCEO members, $35 for nonmembers

- *Incentive Compensation and Employee Ownership* takes a broad look at how companies can use incentives, ranging from stock plans to cash bonuses to gainsharing, to motivate and reward employees.

  $25 for NCEO members, $35 for nonmembers

Other

- *Section 401(k) Plans and Employee Ownership* focuses on how company stock is used in 401(k) plans, both in stand-alone 401(k) plans and combination 401(k)–ESOP plans ("KSOPs").

  $25 for NCEO members, $35 for nonmembers

- *The Ownership Edge* is a handbook for engaging the full entrepreneurial potential of a employee-owned company's workforce through education, information, and engagement.

  $25 for NCEO members, $35 for nonmembers

- *The Journal of Employee Ownership Law and Finance* is the only professional journal solely devoted to employee ownership. Articles are written by leading experts and cover ESOPs, stock options, and related subjects in depth.

  One-year subscription (four issues):
  $75 for NCEO members, $100 for nonmembers

To join the NCEO as a member or to order publications, use the order form on the following page, order online at www.nceo.org, or call us at 510-208-1300. If you join at the same time you order publications, you will receive the members-only publication discounts.

Order Form

This book is published by the National Center for Employee Ownership (NCEO). You can order additional copies online at our Web site, www. nceo.org; by telephoning the NCEO at 510-208-1300; by faxing this page to the NCEO at 510-272-9510; or by sending this page to the NCEO at 1736 Franklin Street, 8th Floor, Oakland, CA 94612. If you join as an NCEO member with this order, or are already an NCEO member, you will pay the discounted member price for any publications you order.

Name

Organization

Address

City, State, Zip (Country)

Telephone   Fax   Email

Method of Payment: ❑ Check (payable to "NCEO")   ❑ Visa   ❑ M/C   ❑ AMEX

Credit Card Number

Signature   Exp. Date

Checks are accepted only for orders from the U.S. and must be in U.S. currency.

Title	Qty.	Price	Total

Tax: California residents add 8.75% sales tax (on publications only, not membership)
Shipping: In the U.S., first publication $5, each add'l $1; elsewhere, we charge exact shipping costs to your credit card, plus a $10 handling surcharge; no shipping charges for membership
Introductory NCEO Membership: $90 for one year ($100 outside the U.S.)

Subtotal	$
Sales Tax	$
Shipping	$
Membership	$
TOTAL DUE	$